# LAW AND CRIMINALITY IN THE MIDDLE AGES

**Hermit Kingdom Studies in
History and Religion 3**

# LAW AND CRIMINALITY IN THE MIDDLE AGES: ACADEMIC ESSAYS

Onyoo Elizabeth Kim

**The Hermit Kingdom Press**
Cheltenham ♦ Seoul ♦ Bangalore ♦ Cebu

## LAW AND CRIMINALITY IN THE MIDDLE AGES: ACADEMIC ESSAYS

Copyright © 2006 by Onyoo Elizabeth Kim

All rights reserved. No part of this book may be reproduced in any form or by any means, electronic or mechanical, including photocopying, recording, or by any information storage and retrieval system (including computer files in any form), without permission in writing from the publisher.

Hardcover: ISBN 1-59689-067-3
Paperback: ISBN 1-59689-068-1
E-Book: ISBN 1-59689-069-X

*Write-To Address:*
The Hermit Kingdom Press
P. O. Box 1226
Highland Park, NJ 08904-1226
United States of America

Hermit Kingdom Studies in History and Religion
ISSN: 1932-6696

---

Library of Congress Cataloging-in-Publication Data

Kim, Onyoo Elizabeth.
 Law and criminality in the middle ages : academic essays / Onyoo Elizabeth Kim.
     p. cm. -- (Hermit Kingdom studies in history and religion ; 3)
 Includes bibliographical references.
 ISBN 1-59689-067-3 (hardcover : alk. paper) -- ISBN 1-59689-068-1 (pbk. : alk. paper)
 1. Law, Medieval. 2. Criminal law--Europe--History--To 1500. 3. Canon law--History--To 1500. I. Title.
 KJ147.K56 2006
 340.5'5--dc22
                                     2006035456

*For my father and mother*

"The problem of the twentieth century is the problem of the color line."

**W. E. B. Du Bois**
*Civil-Rights Leader, 1868-1963*

# Preface

I have been working in the field of medieval history since 1990 when I entered the University of Pennsylvania as an undergraduate history major from the Philadelphia Montgomery Christian Academy in Erdenheim, Pennsylvania, where I was the Co-Valedictorian. The other Co-Valedictorian was Jessalyn Byrd. Jessy also entered the University of Pennsylvania and pursued medieval history. In fact, we were roommates for 3 of the 4 years of our undergraduate education.

During that time, we shared many things – for one, love of kimchee, the quientessential Korean dish made of spicy, pickled cabbage. Besides participating in friendship and in the love of same kinds of cuisine, we worked together as co-editors of the University of Pennsylvania Undergraduate History Journal. After senior year, Jessy took the Thouron Scholarship as the finalist and went on to Oxford University to pursue a D.Phil. in medieval history. I was a semi-finalist of the Thouron Scholarship and that put me on a different path toward law. I headed westward to the UCLA Law School for a Juris Doctor degree.

However, I brought my love of medieval history and in particular medieval law with me. My four years of undergraduate educaton at the

University of Pennsylvania was not a typical undergraduate education. With the guidance of my brother who was a Ph.D. student at UCLA in the history department, I designed a quasi-graduate research program for myself. In fact, I pursued a joint BA-MA degree in medieval history during my four years at PENN. Besides being a history major and getting two degrees in the subject, I also majored in Latin. Having had 4 years of intensive Latin in high school, I was taking doctoral seminars in Latin at PENN by the time I was a junior with graduate students pursuing a Ph.D. in Latin.

My particular thanks are to Professor Edward Peters, my undergraduate history advisor, who guided my masters' thesis on Dante and to Professor James J. O'Donnell of the classics department, who particularly helped my Latin philological skills. Professor O'Donnell has left PENN and now is the Provost of Georgetown University. I would also like to thank Professor E. Ann Matter of the religious studies department at PENN who helped me to acquire different but complementary set of skills (religious studies) than those I acquired primary focusing on the study of history and Latin philology/paleography.

I would also like to thank Professor Manfred Baldus of the University of Cologne Law School in Germany who is one of the leading experts on medieval law in the world, for his kind friendship and encouragement during my research stay in Germany in 2004. I enjoyed our conversations in German and found his doctoral seminar for German doctoral students in medieval law at the University of Cologne helpful in my intellectual development as an expert of medieval law.

I would also like to thank my law students at Handong University Law School in Korea. Teaching law to them has helped me to fine-tune my own ideas on law and criminality. I hope that some of my students at Handong University Law School will go on to pursue medieval law as I have done.

Finally, I would like to thank my family for their continual support and encouragement. My brother Christian has always provided me with constant encouragement and direction. My sister Victoria has always been there when I needed someone to talk to, particularly about the effects of law on society. She is an expert on social welfare policy. And I would like to thank my father Rev. Manwoo A. Kim and my mother Mrs. Sooeun S. Kim for their selfless love and devotion to me. Without their love and encouragement, this book would not have been possible.

Onyoo Elizabeth Kim<br>
Thanksgiving, 2006<br>
Seoul, Korea

# Contents

War and Its Justification
in the Law of the Middle Ages
࿐ 1 ࿐

Understanding "Intent" in Criminal Law
via Gratian's Decretum and St. Augustine
࿐ 49 ࿐

Medieval Canon Law and Sacramental
Theology: The Case of Baptism
࿐ 77 ࿐

The Order of the Templars and their
Criminalization in the 14th Century AD
࿐ 129 ࿐

Understanding the History of Penance
through Medieval Canon Law
࿐ 165 ࿐

# Law and Criminality in the Middle Ages

# WAR AND ITS JUSTIFICATION IN THE LAW OF THE MIDDLE AGES

Underlying the crusading experience is the issue of the legitimacy of the use of force. Rituals surrounding the taking of the cross, which crusades symbolize, emphasize the defensiveness of the expeditions as a justification for the use of force. Different pontifical texts edited by Brundage, Pennington and Pick[1] illustrate that the taking of the cross generally signified the theme of the defense of Christian faith against evil. For example, the text of the Tenth-Century Romano-Germanic Pontifical contains a request to God to bless the wooden cross so that "it would be the comfort and protection and defense against the cruel darts of the enemies."[2] In a thirteenth century English Coventry pontifical, the text is almost identical to the above, except that the

---

[1] The following passages from the texts of pontificals are those edited by these scholars in the appendices of their essays on these pontificals, since I could not obtain either the manuscripts or printed editions.

[2] In Lucy Pick, "*Signaculum Caritatis et Fortitudinis*: Blessing the Crusader's Cross in France," *Revue Benedictine* 105: 3-4 (1995), 381, 411: *Rogamus te, domine sancte, pater omnipotens, aeterne Deus, ut digneris benedicere hoc lignum crucis ut. . . . sit solamen et protectio ac tutela contra seva iacula inimicorum.*

word "sign" (of the cross as a protection and defense against the enemies) is substituted for the "wood" (of the cross).[3] A twelfth-century Italian Lambrecht source also mentions that this sign of the cross provides liberation from enemies and provides a defense from all enemies and treacheries of the devil.[4]

The concept of defense as a main reason for the use of force underwent an evolution in the twelfth and thirteenth centuries. This is apparent when comparing discussions of just war and use of force by two prominent canonists, Gratian in the early twelfth century and Hostiensis in the late thirteenth century. Gratian wrote his monumental piece (the *Concordia Discordantium Canonum*, or *Decretum*) that integrated centuries of ecclesiastical positions on practical issues. In *Causa* 23 of part two of the *Decretum*, Gratian discussed the legitimacy of the use of force against heretical bishops. His emphasis was in justifying certain cases of war, vengeance, killing, and other uses of force against evil and enemies of God, in light of biblical prohibitions against them.[5] On the other hand, Hostiensis

---

[3] In James Brundage, " 'Cruce Signari': The Rite for Taking the Cross in England," *Traditio* 22 (1966), 289, 307: *Rogamus te domine sancte pater omnipotens eterne deus ut benedicere digneris hoc <u>signum</u> tue crucis ut sit. . . . protectio ac tutela contra seva omnium inimicorum iacula* (underscoring mine).

[4] In Kenneth Pennington, "The Rite For Taking the Cross in the Twelfth Century," *Traditio* 30 (1974), 429, 433: *Per signum crucis de inimicis nostris libera nos deus noster. . . . accipe signum crucis Christi. . . . ut sis defensus ab omnibus inimicis tuis et ab omnibus insidiis ipsius diaboli.*

[5] In this case, the pope commanded bishops who received civil jurisdiction from the emperor to defend the Catholics from the

considered just war in the section entitled *treuga et pace* in his *Summa aurea*. He was a diplomat and a canonist, who benefited from canonist activity since Gratian. He divided his presentation into five

---

heretical bishops. These heretics were compelling neighboring Catholics to heresy with threats and tortures, and certain uses of force were applied to them: waging of war, ambushes, execution, plunder of properties, imprisonment, and compulsion to return to the unity of the catholic faith. Gratian then discusses eight questions regarding war, just war, use of arms to avenge the injuries of allies, vengeance, killing by judge or minister, compulsion of evil to good, taking of the property of the heretics, and involvement of bishops and clerics with the use of arms in response to the command of pope or emperor. The Latin text is as follows: *Quidam episcopi cum plebe sibi conmissa in heresim lapsi sunt; circumadiacentes catholicos minis et cruciatibus ad heresim conpellere ceperunt, quo conperto Apostolicus catholicis episcopis circumadiacentium regionum, qui ab inperatore civilem iurisdictionem acceperant, inperavit, ut catholicos ab hereticis defenderent, et quibus modis possent eos ad fidei veritatem redire conpellerent. Episcopi, hec mandata Apostolica accipientes, convocatis militibus aperte et per insidias contra hereticos pugnare ceperunt. Tandem nonnullis eorum neci traditis, aliis rebus suis vel ecclesiasticis expoliatis, aliis carcere et ergastulo reclusis, ad unitatem catholicae fidei coacti redierunt. (Qu. I.) Hic primum queritur, an militare peccatum sit? (Qu. II.) Secundo, quod bellum sit iustum, et quomodo a filiis Israel iusta bella gerebantur? (Qu. III.) Tertio, an iniuria sociorum armis sit propulsanda? (Qu. IV.) Quarto, an vindicta sit inferenda? (Qu. V.) Quinto, an sit peccatum iudici vel ministro reos occidere? (Qu. VI.) Sexto, an malis sint cogendi ad bonum? (Qu. VII.) Septimo, an heretici suis et ecclesiae rebus sint expoliandi, et qui possidet ab hereticis ablata an dicatur possidere aliena? (Qu. VIII.) Octavo, an epicopis vel quibuslibet clericis sua liceat auctoritate, vel apostolici, vel inperatoris precepto arma movere?*

considerations: what is truce, what is peace, what is a just war, how many are the types of truce, how does it operate.[6] Here, he geared towards limiting instances of uses of force.

Comparing the texts of these two canonists and probing the shift, from legitimating to limiting use of force, in the justification of war illuminate different nuances in the use of force. While Gratian focused on the wide jurisdictional authority of the Church and clerics that expanded the possibility of force, Hostiensis specified the secular authorization of the edict of prince, authority of law and of judge to justify war. In addition, Gratian's definition of just war as avenging injuries of God, church and neighbor permitted more opportunity for use of force, while Hostiensis focused on temporal concerns of the recovery of property. Defense of *patria* for the sake of peace had a more spiritual focus for Gratian, and this further increased possibilities for a justified use of force. Finally, Gratian's criteria of intent and agency considerations expanded instantces for the use of force, while Hostiensis' categorizations of just and unjust wars and external criteria of particular limitations (for example, categorizations of war, prohibition against priests and in certain times, issue of restitution) restricted the application of force.

The contexts of the relevant texts illustrate

---

[6] Hostiensis, *Summa aurea*, p. 356: *Quid sit treuga, quid pax, quid sit iustum bellum, de cuius belli treuga hic loquatur, quot sint species treugae, quid operetur.* References to Hostiensis' *Summar aurea* come from the 1963 edition listed in the Bibliography.

the difference in focus between Gratian and Hostiensis. Gratian's support of the use of force is apparent in the context of his discussion. The case scenario itself poses the situation of defending the peace of the church against heretical bishops who initially used force (threats and force) to compel Catholics to heresy and disrupt the unity and peace of the church by urging heretical doctrines. Such scenario allows for, even mandates, a defensive use of force against such people, for a good cause of the church. On the other hand, Hostiensis places his discussion of just war within the section dealing with peace and truce. Such structure underscores the position that war is an aberration from peace which is normative and preferred.

More significantly, comparison of Gratian and Hostiensis' definition of just war indicates their respective emphases. Gratian defined just war, in a dictum in question two, as that which is waged by an edict or which avenges injuries.[7] Hostiensis' definition is similar, but significantly different:

> A just war is that which is waged by the general edict of a prince for the recovery of property. Causa 23. 1. 2....[8]

Gratian simply cites the condition of an edict to

---

[7] C. 23, q. 2, d. p. c. 2: *Cum ergo iustum bellum sit, quod ex edicto geritur, vel quo iniuriae ulciscuntur.*.
[8] Hostiensis, *Summa aurea*, p. 357: *est ergo iustum bellum, quod edicto perpetuo principis geritur de rebus repetendis, aut propulsandorum hominium. Causa. 23. Q. 2....*

justify warfare, while Hostiensis specifies it as an edict *of a prince*. Furthermore, Gratian presents avenging injuries as a condition for a just war, while Hostiensis focuses on the recovery of property. In these variations, Gratian expands the instances of the use of force, while Hostiensis limits them.

Gratian does not specify the nature of the "edict" here, which opens the way for a flexible and expansive concept of authorization of warfare. For Gratian, God is the ultimate authority for the use of force. Those who engage in wars authorized by God, in which killing is inevitably involved, are by no means violating the command, do not kill.[9] Hence, he quotes from Augustine elsewhere that the leader of the army or the people are not the author of war but ministers.[10] The guidance of the Holy Spirit is a source of authority that excuses acts of killing, for example in the case of Samson.[11]

In fact, a limitation on the avenging of injuries is premised on the need to wait for divine punishment in certain situations. Punishment of the evil ones ought to be reserved for God, and they ought not to be punished corporally, although with repeated admonitions and by benefit of charity they ought to be invited to correction.[12] Gratian explains

---

[9] C. 23, q. 5, c. 9: *Qui Deo auctore bella gesserunt, preceptum non occidendi nequaquam transgressi sunt.*
[10] C. 23, q. 2, c. 2: . . . . *in quo bello ductor exercitus vel ipse populus non tam auctor belli, quam minister iudicandus est.*
[11] C. 23, q. 5, c. 9: . . . . *Nec Samson aliter excusatur, quod se ipsum cum hostibus ruina domus obpressit, nisi quia Spiritus latenter hoc iusserat, qui per illum miracula faciebat.* . . .
[12] C. 23, q. 4, d.p. c. 15: *Ex his omnibus colligitur, quod*

that by tolerating the evil ones, it does not mean that they be punished with corporal punishment, but with a spiritual one. When the disciples of Jesus wanted to call down fire from heaven on the Samaritans who did not receive them, Jesus told them, "Do you not know, whose spirit you are. . . . All who receives the sword will die by the sword."[13]

At the same time, the verse, "all who receives the sword will die by the sword" is used to introduce the authority of the church,[14] analogous to the authority of Christ. Under the heading of the one receiving the sword,[15] Gratian quotes from Augustine:

---

*malorum vindicta Deo reservanda est, nec sunt corporaliter puniendi, sed crebra ammonitione, et karitatis beneficio ad correctionem invitandi. Unde Christus ait in evangelio: "Audistis quia dictum est in lege" (quem modum ulcionis lex statuit) "Oculum pro oculo, dentem pro dente." Ego autem hanc vicissitudinem tollens, et ad mansuetudinem et karitatis perfectionem vos invitans, dico vobis: "Nolite resistere malo, sed diligite inimicos vestros, benefacite his, qui oderunt vos,. . . .*

[13] C. 23, q. 4, d.p. c. 12: *Ecce, quod mali tollerandi sunt, nec corporali, sed spirituali vindicta sunt puniendi. Unde, cum discipuli non recepti a Samaritanis ignem celitus super eos deducere voluerunt, dicentes magistra: "vis dicimus descendat ignis de celo, et consumat eos?" audierunt: "Nescitis, cuius spiritus estis?" item, "Omnis, qui gladium acceperit, gladio peribit."*

[14] Gratian's dictum in C. 23, q. 4, d.p. c. 35 (*Item illud evangelii, quod obiciebatur: "Qui gladio usus fuerit gladio cadet," Augustinus exponit in lib. 2. Contra Manicheos, ita dicens:*] precedes c. 36 (*Qui dicatur gladium accipere*) and his dictum following that (see below).

[15] C. 23, q. 4, c. 36: *Qui dicatur gladium accipere.*

> He receives the sword, who is armed in the blood of another with no superior and legitimate power either commanding or granting.[16]

In the dictum following this quote, Gratian comments that the church rationally and justly pursues heretics. The church has the authority of Christ; therefore, its use of force, by its nature, is "just":

> Furthermore that of Jerome, for whom church is denied to pursue someone, is not thus understood, that generally church pursues no one, but that it pursues no one unjustly. For not all pursuit is culpable, but we rationally pursue heretics, just as Christ corporally pursued those whom he expelled from the temple.[17]

Church's use of force is broad, since it is likened to the authority of Christ. This dictum expands the use of force, since despite the fact that Gratian had stated the negative implications of receiving the

---

[16] C. 23, q. 4, c. 36: *Ille gladium accipit, qui, nulla superiori ac legitima potestate vel iubente, vel concedente, in sanguinem alicuius armatur.*

[17] C. 23, q. 4, d.p. c. 36: *Porro illud Ieronimi, quo ecclesia negatur aliquem persequi, non ita intelligendum est, ut generaliter ecclesia nullum persequatur, sed quod nullum iniuste persequatur. Non enim omnis persecutio culpabilis est, sed rationabiliter hereticos persequimur, sicut et Christus corporaliter persecutus est eos, quos de templo expulit.*

sword,[18] the pursuit of heretics by the church is rational and just, analogous to Christ's own example.

In the following canons, Gratian elaborates on the main points of his dictum. The church rationally pursues heretics.[19] The church also seeks help from the kings of the land to pursue the enemies of the church.[20] The church justly pursues evil ones,[21] and by the example of Christ evil ones ought to be compelled to good.[22]

The church not only has authority to directly exercise force, it also can command secular rulers to exercise authority for the interests of the Church. While the churches are not liable to the emperors,[23] the church ought to ask help from the emperor,[24] and catholics can ask for defense against heretics from ordained powers.[25] From the kings of the land the church seeks help against their enemies,[26] and the quietude of the church is helped by the severity

---

[18] C. 23, q. 4, d.p. c. 35: *Item illud evangelii, quod obieciebatur:* "*Qui gladio usus fuerit gladio cadet,*". . . .
[19] C. 23, q. 4, c. 40: *Ecclesia ratione hereticos persequitur.*
[20] C. 23, q. 4, c. 41: *A regibus terrae contra inimicos suos ecclesia auxilium petat.*
[21] C. 23, q. 4, c. 42: *Malos ecclesia iuste persequitur.*
[22] C. 23, q. 4, c. 43: *Exemplo Christi mali sunt ad bonum cogendi.*
[23] C. 23, q. 5, c. 21: *Ecclesiae inperatoribus non sint obnoxiae.*
[24] C. 23, q. 3, c. 2: *Ab inperatore ecclesia auxilium postulare debet.*
[25] C. 23, q. 3, c. 3: *Catholici adversus hereticos a potestatibus ordinatis defensionem postulare possunt.*
[26] C. 23, q. 4, c. 41: *A regibus terrae contra inimicos suos ecclesia auxilium petat.*

of princes.[27]

Furthermore, even though clerics are generally forbidden to shed blood, ecclesiastical leaders have authority to ask secular leaders to help the church, thus expanding the undertaking of force. On the one hand, the role of clerics is in prayer and offering,[28] and priests ought not to take up arms themselves.[29] Priests ought not to be occupied with military business.[30] They who draw the sacraments of the Lord ought not to agitate the judgment of blood.[31] Yet, clerics are permitted to urge others toward snatching arms, defending the oppressed, and fighting the enemies of God.[32] Gratian reiterates this point in a subsequent dictum when he writes that priests, even if they ought not to seize arms with their own hands, nevertheless could persuade others to do so.[33] Also,

---

[27] C. 23, q. 5, c. 4: *Quies ecclesiae principum severitate iuvatur.*
[28] C. 23, q. 8, c. 4: *Pro clerico, qui in bello aut in rixa moritur oratio vel oblatio non offeratur.*
[29] C. 23, q. 8, d.p. c. 6: *His ita respondetur: Sacerdotes propria manu arma arripere non debent....*
[30] C. 23, q. 8, c. 19: *Episcopi non debent militaribus occupari negociis.*
[31] C. 23, q. 8, c. 30: *Non debent agitare iudicium sanguinis qui sacramenta Domini tractant.*
[32] C. 23, q. 8, d.p. c. 6: *His ita respondetur: Sacerdotes propria manu arma arripere non debent; sed alios ad arripiendum, ad oppressorum defensionem, atque ad inimicorum dei oppugnationem eis licet hortari.*
[33] C. 23, q. 8, d.p. c. 18: *. . . . quod sacerdotes, etsi propria manu arma arripere non debeant, tamen vel his, quibus huiusmodi officia conmissa sunt, persuadere, vel quibuslibet, ut ea arripiant, sua auctoritate valeant inperare.*

It is therefore permitted for the prelates of the church, by example of Gregory, to ask the emperors and any leaders for the defense of faith. Also it is permitted. . . . to urge whomever toward their defense against the adversaries of the holy faith. . . .[34]

They can command laymen to act in defense of the church, and this authority over the secular realm removes obstacles for clerics in the use of force.

The role of this secular authority is not just permissible or encouraged; it plays a vital role. Gratian states that priestly admonition does not fare well in correcting those whom secular power corrects.[35] It is the office of kings to compress the evil ones and lift up the good ones.[36]

Both kingly authority and priestly authority defend that which pertains to the divine confession.[37] He is defrauded of eternal reward who shows contempt in preserving faith and reverence

---

[34] C. 23, q. 8, d.p. c. 28: *Licet ergo prelatis ecclesiae exemplo B. Gregorii ab inperatoribus vel quibuslibet ducibus defensionem fidelibus postulare. Licet etiam. . . . quoslibet ad sui defensionem contra adversarios sanctae fidei viriliter adhortari. . . .*
[35] C. 23, q. 5, c. 22: *Sacerdotalis ammonitio quos corrigere non valet secularis potentia corrigat.*
[36] C. 23, q. 5, c. 23: *Malos conprimere, et bonos sublevare regum officium est.*
[37] C. 23, q. 5, c. 21: *Et regia, et sacerdotalis defendant auctoritas que ad divinam confessionem pertinent.*

by these powers.³⁸ Gratian says in a dictum that "from these princes and powers it is necessary that faith and reverence be preserved, which he who will not exhibit before God could not find award."³⁹ Moreover, just as to princes and powers one is forced to exhibit faith and reverence, so the necessity of defending churches presses upon the administers of secular dignities. But if they disregard to do so, they ought to be repelled from the communion.⁴⁰ Secular princes ought not to spare the worst.⁴¹ Injury of the sacraments of Christ ought to be punished by kings.⁴² Hidden and other crimes ought to be repressed by the king.⁴³ Those divided from the unity of the church ought to be coerced by secular authorities.⁴⁴ The secular powers also have authority to use force to deal with schismatics and heretics.⁴⁵ Sins are punished by

---

³⁸ C. 23, q. 5, c. 24: *Eterna mercede fraudatur qui fidem et reverentiam potestatibus servare contempnit.*

³⁹ C. 23, q. 5, d.p. c. 23: *Ipsis autem principibus et potestatibus fidem et reverentiam servari oportet, quam qui non exhibuerit apud Deum premia invenire non poterit.*

⁴⁰ C. 23, q. 5, d.p. c. 25: *Preterea, sicut principibus et potestatibus fidem et reverentiam exhibere cogimur, ita secularium dignitatum amministratoribus defendendarum ecclesiarum necessitas incumbit. Quod si facere contempserint, a communione sunt repellendi.*

⁴¹ C. 23, q. 5, c. 32: *Principes seculi pessimis parcere non debent.*

⁴² C. 23, q. 5, c. 34: *Iniuria sacramentorum Christi a regibus est vindicanda.*

⁴³ C. 23, q. 5, c. 40: *Furta et cetera crimina a rege sunt cohibenda.*

⁴⁴ C. 23, q. 5, c. 44: *Ab ecclesiae unitate divisi a secularibus potestatibus coherceantur.*

⁴⁵ C. 23, q. 5, c. 43: *Scismaticos et hereticos seculi potestates*

people, not necessarily people of God, spurred by divine command.[46] Even those ignorant of God are used as divine tools to punish the sins of the Israelites, for example, King Sennacherib of Assyria and Nabuchodonosor of Babylonia.[47]

Secular rulers also have a positive mandate to engage in uses of force to protect the weak. Emperors, with the provision of bishops of church, ought to undertake defense against the power of the rich.[48] The expansion of legitimate instances of force under Gratian's approach exists not only in ecclesiastical authority and jurisdiction over the secular sphere but in the secular rulers' duty from heaven to specifically serve and protect the interests of the church, such as defending the sacrament, faith and reverence, unity of Church, and peace of church against heretics and schismatics and criminals. The authority of the secular rulers, then, demands responsibility owed to the church, not confer superior powers.

On the other hand, Hostiensis's conception

---

coherceant.
[46] C. 23, q. 5, c. 49: *Aliquando puniuntur peccata per populos divino iussu excitatos.*
[47] C. 23, q. 5, d.p. c. 49: *Hinc notandum est, quod aliquando punit Deus peccata per nescientes, aliquando per scientes. Per nescientes peccata punit, sicut per Sennacherib, et per Nabuchodonosor, et per Antiochum, et per principes Romanorum, et per nonnullos reges gentilium populum Israeliticum delinquentem afflixit aliquando, aliquando captivavit.*
[48] C. 23, q. 3, c. 10: *Inperatores cum episcoporum provisione ecclesiae defensionem adversus divitum potenciam debent suscipere.*

of authority for the use of force is more temporal in origin and goal. He specifies the edict to be that of a prince, in his definition of a just war.[49] Centrality of secular authority in a just war is apparent in the next sentence:

> briefly, he who by his judge's authority rightly intervening, receives the sword, whether of one commanding, or of one consenting, it is just.[50]

While Gratian uses the language *vel iubente, vel concedente* to introduce the expansive scope of church authority and focus on the justness factor from the side of the church,[51] Hostiensis employs similar language of *sive iubentis, sive consentientis* to define and limit those instances where use of force is just.

In fact for Hostiensis, the church, which is pure, is not allowed to shed blood, either through itself or through another.[52] Whereas clerics and holy men, for Gratian, are not "shedding blood" when they urge others to snatch arms, Hostiensis states that clerics, either in their own persons *or*

---

[49] Hostiensis, *Summa aurea*, p. 357: *est ergo iustum bellum, quod edicto perpetuo principis geritur de rebus repetendis, aut propulsandorum hominium.*

[50] Hostiensis, *Summa aurea*, p. 357: . . . . *Iustum.* . . . *et breviter, qui authoritate sui iudicis recte interveniente, accipit gladium, sive iubentis, sive consentientis, iustum est. 23.q. 3.*

[51] *Supra*, n. 16.

[52] Hostiensis, *Summa aurea*, p. 367: . . . . *ut puta quia ecclesiastica est, cui non est licitum effundere sanguinem nec per se, ne per alium.*

through others, should not shed blood. This difference is a further evidence of Gratian's efforts to legitimate, and Hostiensis' focus to limit, uses of force.

Furthermore, Hostiensis limits instances of force by grounding the centrality of authority less in a spiritual sense. Rather, he states that a war is waged "either by the authority of the judge, by the authority of the law, or by one's own will."[53] In his seven categorizations of just and unjust wars, the criterion of justness of warfare is determined by whether it is with the authority of a judge or of law, or not.[54] Focusing on the temporal source of authority contrasts from Gratian's divine authority of the church to pursue its enemies in many possible cases.

The purpose of a just war also differs in emphasis between Gratian and Hostiensis. Gratian defines a just war as that which avenges injuries, while Hostiensis replaces it with the recovery of property. It becomes apparent that by injuries, Gratian means those of the church, committed against God and neighbor. For Hostiensis, the focus of the goal of a just war is a limited one of defense of *patria* and paternal laws. These variations further illustrate the expansiveness of the use of force in Gratian's discussion on the one hand, as opposed to a limitation in Hostiensis' position.

Gratian, citing from Augustine in question 2, defines a just war as an avenue for avenging injuries

---

[53] Hostiensis, *Summa aurea*, pp. 358-59: *quia aut fit authoritate iudicis, aut authoritate iuris, aut propria voluntate.*
[54] Hostiensis, *Summa aurea*, pp. 359-60.

(*ulciscuntur iniurias*),

> which ought to be sought, where a nation and people neglected to vindicate what was done wickedly by them, or neglected to return that which was taken away through injuries. But this type of war is without doubt just, which God commands, who knew what ought to be done for him; in which war the leader of the army or the people itself ought to be judged no more the author of war as the minister of war.[55]

Gratian provides the example of the sons of Israel who waged a just war against the Amorites in order to avenge their injuries, since the Amorites refused them passage through their land.[56] The denial of a harmless crossing to the Israelites was an injury, "which by the law of human society ought to be accessible most equally."[57] Hence Israel had the right

---

[55] C. 23, q. 2, c. 2: *Iusta autem bella solent diffiniri, que ulciscuntur iniurias, sic gens et civitas, petenda est, que vel vindicare neglexerit quod a suis inprobe factum est vel reddere quod per iniurias ablatum est. Sed et hoc genus bellis sine dubio iustum est, quod Deus inperat, qui, novit quid cuique fieri debeat; in quo bello ductor exercitus vel ipse populus non tam auctor belli, quam minister iudicandus est.*

[56] C. 23, q. 2, d.p. c.2: *Cum ergo iustum bellum sit, quod ex edicto geritur, vel quo iniuriae ulciscuntur, queritur, quomodo a filiis Israel iusta bella gerebantur*, C. 23, q. 2, c. 3: *Innoxius transitus filiis Israel negabatur, atque ideo iusta bella gerebantur.*

[57] C. 23, q. 2, c. 3: *Innoxius enim transitus negabatur, qui iure*

to wage a just war. In focusing on the avenging of injuries, Gratian gives an example of a subjective justification ("law of human society") which has a potential for expanding the category for permissible uses of force.

This key concept of avenging injuries occurs in question four dealing with the legitimacy of vengeance, or punishment for injuries, which further illustrates Gratian's concern to legitimate uses of force. At first, he starts out with the general proposition that vengeance ought not to be inflicted but that evil ones ought to be tolerated, not thrown down; struck by scolding, not by corporal banishment.[58] Furthermore, personal injury standing alone does not comprise a legitimate case for the use of force or vengeance. Regarding the Old Testament law of personal avenging (*lex ulcionis*), Jesus emphasized the new law of bearing the hatred of enemies with love.[59] Gratian then quotes from other areas of the Bible to support this. Gratian's exposition of a commonly used example of the disciples' wanting to call down fire from heaven on the Samaritans illustrates the inadequacy of

---

*humanae societatis equissimo patere debebat.*
[58] C. 23, q. 4, d.a. c. 1: *Quod autem vindicta inferenda non sit, multis modis probatur. Mali enim tollerandi sunt, non abiciendi; increpatione feriendi, non corporaliter expellendi.*
[59] C. 23, q. 4, d.p. c. 15: . . . .*Unde Christus ait in evangelio: "Audistis quia dictum est in lege" (quem modum ulcionis lex statuit) "Oculum pro oculo, dentem pro dente." Ego autem hanc vicissitudinem tollens, et ad mansuetudinem et karitatis perfectionem vos invitans, dico vobis: "Nolite resistere malo, sed diligite inimicos vestros, benefacite his, qui oderunt vos,. . . .*

personal injuries for revenge:

> The apostles, not by zeal of justice but by hate of *bitterness on account of injury of their expulsion* wished to consume the Samaritans by fire. The Lord, moreover, wishing that they *tolerate the injury to their own person* with patience and joy, not to leave the injury of divine service unavenged, said, "you do not know, whose spirit you are?" Here also Peter, who, when he heard others, "blessed will you be when men say evil of you and they said all evil against you; rejoice on that day, and rejoice, since your abundance is in heaven...."[60]

Following this dictum, Gratian cites Gregory: on account of one's own injury it is not permitted for

---

[60] C. 23, q. 4, d.p. c. 26: *Potest in hac prohibitione Apostolorum alius intelligi. Apostoli non zelo iusticiae, sed amaritudinis odio ob iniuriam suae expulsionis vindicandam Samaritanos igne voluerunt consumere; Dominus autem volens eos iniuriam propriae personae cum patiencia et gaudio tollerare, iniuriam vero servitutis divinae non inultam relinquere, ait: "Nescitis, cuius spiritus esti?" Hinc etiam Petrus, qui, cum aliis audierat: "Beati eritis, cum maledixerint vobis homines, et dixerint omne malum adversus vos; gaudete in illa die, et exultate, quoniam merces vestra copiosa est in celis,"....* (italics in the English translation are mine).

the bishop to excommunicate someone.[61]

Although personal injury is not a legitimate basis for punishment, revenge and excommunication, sins, which are committed against God or against neighbor, ought to be punished by us, although those committed against us ought to be tolerated patiently or rather ignored.[62] Then Gratian emphasizes that it is the injury of the church, not that of one's own, that was avenged.[63]

Avenging injury to the peace of the church is a core issue in Gratian's lengthy discussion of force in *Causa* 23, which presents the danger posed against the unity and peace of the church by heretical bishops who first used threats and force to compel Catholics to heresy and urge heretical doctrines. In some circumstances, peace of the church determines the abstaining from force. Evil ones ought to be tolerated[64] for the purpose of preserving the peace of the church.[65] Where the church receives and not expels the evil ones, they ought to be tolerated by the good people.[66] Gratian reasons that good ones cannot be completely

---

[61] C. 23, q. 4, c. 27: *Pro iniuria propria episcopo aliquem excommunicare non licet.*

[62] C. 23, q. 4, d.p. c. 27: *Hinc idem in omeliis, ostendens, quod peccata, que in Deum vel in proximum conmittuntur, a nobis punienda sunt, ea vero, quibus in nos delinquitur, patienter tolleranda, vel potius dissimulanda sunt ait.*

[63] C. 23, q. 4, d. p. c. 30: *Sed et hic non suam, sed ecclesiae iniuriam ultus est.*

[64] C. 23, q. 4, c. 2: *Quod mali sint tollerandi a bonis.*

[65] C. 23, q. 4, c. 3: *Pro pace ecclesiae mali sunt tollerandi.*

[66] C. 23, q. 4, c. 11: *Mali, quos ecclesia recipit, nec expellit, a bonis sunt tollerandi.*

separated from the evil ones in this life,[67] and the present church receives the good and the evil similarly,[68] so they are to be tolerated.

Furthermore, toleration of potentially dangerous elements by the good is due to the fact that the evil one does not defile you if you do not consent to him but disprove of him.[69] As long as you do not touch the impure, you do not consent to sins.[70] The deeds of the harmful do not defile the innocent who do not believe those deeds.[71] In addition, Gratian applies the theology of predestination and free will: for some, correction by words or flogging is not useful and superfluous, since the predestined are changed to life without correction, just as Peter, whom the Lord's gaze moved him to tears. In contrast was Pharaoh who went to his death despite many whippings.[72]

On the other hand, promoting the peace of

---

[67] C. 23, q. 4, c. 14: *Boni a malis numquam in hac vita penitus possunt separari.*
[68] C. 23, q. 4, c. 15: *Presens ecclesia simul recipit bonos et malos.*
[69] C. 23, q. 4, c. 8: *Non te maculat malus, si ei non consentis, sed ipsum redarguis.*
[70] C. 23, q. 4, c. 9: *Inmundum tangere est peccatis consentire.*
[71] C. 23, q. 4, c. 10: *Non maculant innocentes facta nocentium, que ab eis credi non possunt.*
[72] C. 23, q. 4, d. p. c. 19: *Est etiam alia causa, qua correctio verborum vel verberum videtur esse inutilis vel superflua. Predestinati enim ad vitam sine correctione mutantur, sicut Petrus, quem Dominus respiciens nemine corripiente conmovit ad lacrimas. Presciti ad mortem inter flagella deteriores fiunt, sicut Pharao. Bonis ergo superflua, dampnandis inveniuntur hec esse inutilia. His ita respondetur auctoritate Gregorii et Augustini.*

the church, in more instances, mandates an action of force to avenge injuries against God and neighbor whom the church has interest to protect. He who does not repel injury from his ally is similar to the one who inflicts injury.[73] He who ceases to oppose them supports the impiety of the evil ones.[74] Those who are contemptuous of the divine command are in turn legitimate objects of the most severe vengeance.[75] Secular rulers serve the interests of the church by their use of force at the church's request. Quietude, or peace, of the church is helped by severity of princes. In fact, the peace of the church alleviates the gloominess of the perpetrators.[76]

Closely related to the peace of church is the concept of *patria*, which for Gratian pertains to the spiritual realm (church) and matters (defending faith against heretics, defense of the weak and poor). When Gratian mentions *patria* in the context of the legitimacy of waging wars, he quotes Ambrose to state that complete justice is that which protects the *patria* from barbarians by war.[77] *Patria*, in this context, refers to the church and the neighbors the church encouraged to protect, such as the weak, poor, and others. The cited passage of Ambrose

---

[73] C. 23, q. 3, c. 7: *Qui a socio non repellit iniuriam similis est ei, qui facit.*
[74] C. 23, q. 3, c. 8: *Malorum inpietati favet qui eis obviare cessat.*
[75] C. 23, q. 3, c. 9: *Qui divina mandata contempnunt severis coherceantur vindictis.*
[76] C. 23, q. 5, c. 48: *Pax ecclesiae mesticiam consolatur perditorum.*
[77] C. 23, q. 3, c. 5: *Iustiticia plenus est qui patriam bello tuetur a barbaris.*

includes the protection of the weak at home, or of friends from thieves.[78] Thieves and pirates weaken the members of the church.[79] In such cases, the use of force is justified and necessary for good. Stating that to war is not sin,[80] Gratian cites Augustine to support his point that pacified wars are those which are waged so that the evil ones are coerced and the good men are lifted up.[81]

Although Hostiensis, like Gratian, considers *patria* as a significant factor to justify war, his definition of a just war as an edict of a prince and for the recovery of property sheds a different nuance to *patria* that in effect limits uses of force. For Hostiensis, *patria* is temporal in nature. Hostiensis states that a just war is that which is waged by a leader on behalf of one's own defense, whether of his own fatherland or of paternal laws.[82] Likewise, on behalf of own, and for defense of own fatherland or of paternal laws and for peace, justice ought to be defended.[83] Hostiensis' focus for a just

---

[78] C. 23, q. 3, c. 5: *Fortitudo, que bello tuetur a barbaris patriam, vel domi defendit infirmos, vel a latronibus socios, plena iustitia est.*
[79] C. 23, q. 3, c. 6: *Prodest latroni vel piratae qui membra eius debilitat.*
[80] C. 23, q. 1, c. 5: *Militare non est peccatum.*
[81] C. 23, q. 1, c. 6: *Pacata sunt bella, que geruntur, ut mali coherceantur et boni subleventur.*
[82] Hostiensis, *Summa aurea*, p. 356: *Quid sit iustum bellum. . . . Dicit decretum quod militare peccatum non est. 23. 1. I. Militare. Quod verum est, si a principe indicatur, ut sequitur. . . . Similiter pro defensione sua, seu patriae suae, vel legum paternarum.*
[83] Hostiensis, *Summa aurea*, p. 357: *Item pro sua, & patriae suae seu legum paternarum defensione, et pace, iustitia*

war is not avenging ecclesiastical injuries so much as for recovering the safety of the fatherland and paternal laws. Furthermore, temporal peace, as absence of war, is of prime importance. Hence Hostienis writes that "breaker or violator of peace ought to be excommunicated, according to the canons. . . . but according to the law, he ought to be executed."[84] He urges obtaining of truce in these circumstances.[85] War is not waged so that peace is acquired,[86] whereas for Gratian, force is used to preserve the peace of the church.

This contrasts from Gratian who urged force even at the expense of temporal peace, with any means, in order to promote the "peace of the church" that justifies use of force. Hostiensis has a more mundane conception of peace, related to *treuga*, or truce. In the beginning of his discussion on *treuga et pace*, he states that peace is limited discord and called truce."[87] It is "security maintained for a time for persons and things, discord not yet finished, because in law it is called treaty or armistice."[88]

---

*tuenda*. . . .

[84] Hostiensis, *Summa aurea*, p. 352: *Fractor seu violator pacis excommunicandus est, secundum canones. . . . sed secundum leges capite puniendus.*

[85] Hostiensis, *Summa aurea*, p. 361: *treugam firmiter observandam.*

[86] Hostiensis, *Summa aurea*, p. 361: . . . . *bellum non geritur, ut pax acquiratur.*

[87] Hostiensis, *Summa aurea*, p. 356.

[88] Hostiensis, *Summa aurea*, p. 356: *securitas personis, et rebus ad tempus praestita, discordia nondum finita, quod in lege dicitur foedus vel inducia.* . . .

For Gratian, the justness of the use of force not only depends on avenging injuries of church by the authority of church, but it also derives its legitimacy from proper intent. From the beginning of his discussion on the use of force, Gratian cites Augustine and focuses on the criterion of intent for measuring the legitimacy of conduct. In response to question one, whether it is sin to wage war, Gratian poses a statement from Augustine that the precepts of patience, not so much the show of body than the preparation of the heart, ought to be retained.[89] This statement is reiterated at the end of his discussion of question one to show that waging war may not be sin.[90] This use of *preparatione cordis* shows instances where war is not sin; in fact, this factor necessitates wars in certain cases, provided that the motive is not selfishness or desire for loot but a genuine concern for the unity of the church and turning evil to good and protecting the weak.

In question four, Gratian argues that although it is generally not legitimate to exercise vengeance, it is proper and necessary when the motivation is that of love, as in the case of Moses. Gratian states that when Moses whipped the people, it was not out of cruelty but out of love.[91] The end

---

[89] C. 23, q. 1, d.p. c.1: *Precepta patienciae non tam ostentatione corporis quam preparatione cordis sunt retinenda.*
[90] C. 23, q. 1, d.p. c. 7: *Ex his omnibus colligitur, quod militare non est peccatum, et quod precepta patienciae in preparatione cordis, non ostentatione corporis servanda sunt.*
[91] C. 23, q. 4, c. 44: *Non crudelitate, sed dilectione Moyses populum flagellavit.*

of Gratian's discussion of vengeance emphasizes the right intent of vengeance, which is charity:

> From all these it is concluded, that vengeance, ought to be inflicted, not by love of vengeance itself, but by zeal of justice; not so that hate is exercised, but so that crookedness is corrected. But when sometimes vengeance is inflicted for damages of things, sometimes by whips, sometimes by death, it is asked, whether it is sin for a judge or a minister to commit victims to death?[92]

Gratian quotes Augustine to conclude his discussion of the use of force, when he states that a man ought to love his neighbor, just as himself.[93] In this discussion of vengeance in question four, Gratian begins and ends with Augustine and the overarching principle of charity. This principle of charity that generally prohibits uses of force such as war, vengeance, and killing justifies and demands a certain use of such force. Gratian employs an Augus-

---

[92] C. 23, q. 4, d.p. c. 53: *Ex his omnibus colligitur, quod vindicta est inferenda non amore ipsius vindictae, sed zelo iusticiae; non ut odium exerceatur, sed ut pravitas corrigatur. Sed cum vindicta aliquando inferatur dampnis rerum, aliquando flagellis, aliquando etiam morte: queritur, an sit peccatum iudici vel ministro reos morti tradere?*

[93] C. 23, q. 4, c. 53: *Quemadmodum homo debet diligere proximum sicut se ipsum.*

tinian balance of love and war to legitimate force in order to preserve the unity of the Christian faith.

On the other hand, for Hostiensis, regardless of religious intent and goal and the action by the faithful, a war is legitimate only if it meets specified criteria for a just war. Proper authority, not necessarily the church, must sanction war, as his seven categories of wars illustrate. The first category of Roman war, in which the faithful wage war against the unfaithful, is just. But wars fought by the faithful are not *per se* just. The second category names another just war, the judicial war where the faithful, by the authority of the judge, wage war. In contrast, war waged by the faithful contumaciously opposing the judge is a presumptuous war and unjust (third one). The fourth type is one authorized by law, and therefore permissible and just. On the other hand, war waged by the faithful against the authority of law is rash and unjust (fourth). War waged on one's own authority is the sixth kind which is willful and unjust, while war waged by the faithful in self-defense permitted by the authority of law against those attacking by volition is necessary and just (seventh).[94]

---

[94] Hostiensis, *Summa aurea*, pp. 359-60: *In summa praedicta recolligamus, alius potest dici bellum Romanum, puta quod est inter fideles et infideles, et hoc iustum. . . . Unum. Hoc autem voco Romanum, quia Roma est caput fidei nostrae. . . . Secundum, quod est inter fideles pugnantes authoritate iudicis, et hoc iudiciale potest dici, et est iustum. . . . Tertium, quod faciunt fideles iudici contumaces, et potest vocari praesumptuosum, et est iniustum. . . . Quartum, quod faciunt fideles authoritate iuris, et hoc potest dici licitum, et est*

The Roman war at first seems to coincide with Gratian's expansion of force for spiritual and ecclesiastical concerns. The Roman war is one in which the faithful ones wage war against the unfaithful, who rupture the bond of faith in Christian society. Hostiensis states that amid multiple wars, such war between the faithful and the unfaithful is just with respect to the faithful.[95] Furthermore, Hostiensis states that this war ought not to be abstained in any day, because truce restrictions do not apply to a Roman war.[96] This seems to suggest that Hostiensis considers this war unconditionally just.

However, Hostiensis actually places restrictions even with respect to this war, thus limiting instances of force more emphatically than Gratian. In order to qualify for the use of force under the first category, the war must be a Roman war in the first place and not fall under the five characterizations of an unjust war:

> Nevertheless there are those who say that unjust war is assessed in five ways: First, the war of Roman matter,

---

*iustum. Quintum quod faciunt fideles contra authoritate iuris, et hoc potest dici temerarium, et est iniustum. . . . Sextum, quod faciunt fideles propria authoritate, alios impugnantes, et hoc potest dici voluntarium, et est iniustum. Septimum, quod fideles faciunt defendendo se authoritate iuris contra voluntatem impugnantes, et hoc potest dici necessarium, et est iustum.*

[95] Hostiensis, *Summa aurea*, pp. 358-59: *Unum, quod est inter fideles et infideles, et hoc iustum est respectu fidelium.*
[96] Hostiensis, *Summa aurea*, p. 360-61.

> as if not for the recovery of property or on behalf of the defense of fatherland. . . . Second, the war of Roman cause as if voluntarily, the war would not be fought by necessity. . . . Third, from the spirit. . . . .when the war would be waged for revenge. . . . Fourth, if it would not be waged by authority of the prince. . . . Fifth, by reason of person, since the church is pure, for which it is not permitted that blood pours out either through itself, nor through another.[97]

Even in the war of Roman matter and cause, five qualities will render a war unjust. Recovery of property is a significant element, as is the defense of fatherland and necessity. Hence, if war is not for the recovery of property or on behalf of the defense of the fatherland, it is not a justified war. Volition is also not sufficient; necessity must compel the just war. Also, in contrast to Gratian's exceptions for use of vengeance, Hostiensis treats it as a factor invalidating a war on unjust grounds. Authority of the prince is a further requirement of Hostiensis, and church shall not pour blood either through itself

---

[97] Hostiensis, *Summa aurea*, p. 357: *Sunt tamen qui dicunt bellum iniustum censeri quinque modis. Primo, romanae rei, ut si non est de repetendis rebus vel pro defensione patriae. . . . Secundo, Romanae causae ut si voluntarie, non necessario pugnetur. . . . Tertio, ex animo. . . .. quando fiat ad vindictam. . . . . Quarto, si non fit authoritate principis. . . . . Quinto, ratione personae, ut puta quia ecclesiastica est, cui non est licitum effundere sanguinem nec per se, ne per alium.*

*or* through another, in contrast to Gratian's providing for the churchmen's capacity to urge laymen and command secular leaders.

The criterion of authority in the categorization of wars and the characterization of unjust wars in effect limit force, and render it not as a positive duty in the sacred use of force, but as a default mechanism of a last resort. In his discussion of clerics and violence, Hostiensis also includes a canonist opinion that "in inevitable necessity just on behalf of self, not for others, they can take up all weapons for defending: but if otherwise they can avoid they should not take up [arms]."[98] This reflects Hostiensis' general attitude and emphasis in limiting the use of force, defensive as it may be. Similarly, regarding the waging of unjust war, Hostiensis writes that "if no inevitable necessity urges, or unfitness likewise could be understood regarding the unjust war, then it ought not to be waged in any time."[99]

Observation of truce further limits occasions of force. Certain periods of truce applied to all types of wars except the Roman war:

> Regarding truce of war here discussed does not apply to the Roman

---

[98] Hostiensis, *Summa aurea*, p. 357: *Alii dicunt, quod in necessitate inevitabili pro se tantum, non pro aliis ad defendendum possunt omnia arma sumere: sed si aliter possunt evadere, non sumant.*

[99] Hostiensis, *Summa aurea*, pp. 360-61: *si inevitabilis urget necessttas, vel importunitas idem potest intelligi de iniusto bello, quod et si nullo tempore. . . .*

one, since it ought not to be abstained in any day. . . . but does apply to war which is not licit, nor necessary, since necessity would not substitute for law. . . . If, moreover, you understand this regarding the unjust or voluntary war, this ought not to be waged in any time. . . . This could be understood regarding the just war, it could be understood that one ought not to cease from it in any time, but one ought to vacate less in these times and days. . . . this likewise gives approval to this Decretum, when he says, if no inevitable necessity urges, or unfitness likewise could be understood regarding the unjust war, then it ought not to be waged in any time, nevertheless less in these times and days than others. It could, therefore, be understood regarding the judicial, licit, indistinct and voluntary, not presumptuous and rash, that the pope, on account of this, moreover does not wish to approve such kind of war: but since and if in whole it cannot be corrected, men will be controlled from either side.[100]

---

[100] Hostiensis, *Summa aurea*, pp. 360-61: *De cuius belli treuga hic loquitur de romano non, quia ab illo nulla die abstinendum est. . . . quod non est licitum, nec necessario, quia necessitas legi non subiacet. . . . Si autem hoc intelligas de iniusto. . . . voluntario, hoc nullo tempore faciendum est. . . . Potest hoc intelligi de iusto bello, a quo et si nullo tempore sit*

This passage shows how unjust wars ought not to be waged at all (*quod et si nullo tempore faciendum est*), and even the just ones, with the exception of the first one, cannot be waged in times of truce.

Rules regarding truce tremendously restrict the use of force. Quoting from the *Innovamus* decretal, Hostiensis includes the fact that canonical truce is held in perpetuity for certain people and beasts: clerics, monks, lay brothers, pilgrims and farmers and all living creatures and servants of the farms while they are in agriculture. As long as the farmers are in agriculture and clerics and monks live in churches, they enjoy this privilege.[101]

---

*cessandum, minus tamen ei vacandum est his temporibus, et diebus de quibus haec decreta supponit et hoc idem innuit illud decretum, si nulla, cum dicit, si inevitabilis urget necessitas, vel importunitas idem potest intelligi de iniusto bello, quod et si nullo tempore faciendum est, minus tamen his temporaribus, et diebus quam aliis. Potest ergo intelligi de iudiciali, et licito, indistincte, et de voluntario, non praesumptuoso, et temerario, non tamen quod papa propter hoc approbare velit tale bellum: sed quia et si in totum corrigi non possit, homines refraenentur utrinque.*

[101] Hostiensis, *Summa aurea*, p. 361: *Item canonica est illa treuga, de qua hic loquitur, et istam aliquid habent perpetuam, aliqui temporalem. Perpetuam habent clerici, monachi, conversi, peregrini, et rustici cum animalibus et ministris omnibus rusticanis, dum sunt in agricultura, et redeunt, et vadunt. . . . innovamus. . . . habent autem hoc privilegium rustici, quamdiu fuerint in agricultura, sicut milites, dum militant. . . . sic clerici, et monachi, et conversi, dum in ecclesiis. . . . vivunt, gaudent privilegio clericali. . . . Sic legati gaudent privilegio, dum in legatione constistunt. . . . Sicut et animalia, quae ad agriculturam pertinent. Si vero cum laicis communem vitam suscipiunt, merito cum eisdem communem*

From another canon, *Treugas autem* of the Third Lateran Council, Hostiensis considers truce for certain days, which further limits uses of force. For example, from Thursday, setting of the day, to Tuesday, before the rising of the sun, on Friday on account of the Ascension of the Lord, on Saturday on account of the Passion of the Lord, on Sabbath day, or Sunday, on account of the Resurrection, Advent and Lent seasons, all truces are to be observed. The consequence of failing to keep the truce is excommunication of the diocese.[102]

Hostiensis' detailed criterion for just war, as well as the prescribed consequences for waging an unjustified war, therefore restricts instances of sacred violence. It is not the subjective evaluations of the agent's intent but the objective and specified criteria that must be met for a war to be justified in the eyes of the law.

Besides intent, justness of certain uses of force also derives from legitimacy of the capacity

---

*in legibus sentient disciplinam.*
[102] Hostiensis, *Summa aurea*, p. 361: *Temporalem vero habent omnes communiter, et durat a quarta seria post occasum solis, usque ad secundam seriam ante ortum solis, seria quinta, propter Ascensionem Domini, seria sexta propter Domini passionem, die Sabbati, via dies est requiei. Die Dominica, propter Resurrectionem. Item ab adventu Domini usque ad octavas Epiphaniae, et septuagesima usque octavas Paschae. . . . ad has treugas observandas, tres funiculi colliguntur, dioecesanorum excommunicatio, confirmatio. . . . conprobatio, similis expositio. . . . . Sed quaeritur, an episcopi constituantur transgressores, si hoc non servent. Et potest dici, quod non, eo quod non sunt haec moribus utentium approbata.*

for action, the concept of agency. A murderer is one who, *not* having a public function, kills or debilitates someone.[103] However, those who engage in justified force are acting within the capacity of law. The leader of the army ought to be judged not the author of war but a minister of war.[104] Those who wage wars with God as author by no means transgress the precept of do not kill,[105] since from the office it is not sin to kill a man.[106] Those in the Old Testament who killed the "evil" ones were not transgressors of law but defenders, because the law kills, and the person doing the killing is only an agent not legally responsible for killing.[107] The soldier is not accused of homicide when he kills a man in obedience to power.[108] One who spontaneously kills those whom the judge commands to be killed is not guilty of homicide.[109] The faithful, who either exercise torments or carry out capital punishment within their office, are not to be

---

[103] C. 23, q. 8, c. 33: *Homicida est, qui, publicam functionem non habens, aliquem occidit aut debilitat.*
[104] C. 23, q. 2, c. 2: . . . . *in quo bello ductor exercitus vel ipse populus non tam auctor belli, quam minister iudicandus est.*
[105] C. 23, q. 5, c. 9: *Qui Deo auctore bella gesserunt, preceptum non occidendi nequaquam transgressi sunt.*
[106] C. 23, q. 5, c. 8: *Ex officio non est peccatum hominem occidere.*
[107] C. 23, q. 5, d.p. c. 7: . . . . *Similiter nonnulli in veteri testamento inveniuntur malos trucidasse, nec transgressores legis, sed defensores appellantur.*
[108] C. 23, q. 5, c. 13: *Non est reus homicidii miles, qui potestati obediens hominem occidit.*
[109] C. 23, q. 5, c. 14: *Homicida est qui sponte occidit quo iudex iubet occidi.*

blamed.[110] Hence, a dictator is immune from blame when the authority of laws is exercised against the rebellious.[111] He who punishes the murderer and the sacrilegious sheds no blood.[112] Those armed against the excommunicates out of zeal for the mother church are not murderers.[113] When holy men and public powers wage wars, they have not in fact shed blood when they punish in the capacity as minister of laws, since evil men are not only to be flagellated but killed.[114] He who dutifully kills the one causing harm is not sinning.[115] Gratian then cites from Augustine that ends with, "when a man is killed by law justly, the law kills, not you."[116]

In fact, it is not cruelty but piety to punish

---

[110] C. 23, q. 4, c. 45: *Non inputatur fidelibus, qui ex officio aut tormenta exercent, aut capitalem sentenciam ferunt.*

[111] C. 23, q. 4, c. 46: *Inmunis est dictator a culpa, cum legum auctoritas in inprobos exercetur.*

[112] C. 23, q. 5, c. 31: *Non sanguinem fundit qui homicidas et sacrilegos punit.*

[113] C. 23, q. 5, c. 47: *Non sunt homicidae qui adversus excommunicatos zelo matris ecclesiae armantur.*

[114] C. 23, q. 5, c. 48: *Si ergo viri sancti et publicae potestates bella gerentes non fuerunt transgressores illius mandati: "non occides" quamvis quosque flagitiosus digna morte perimerent; si miles suae potestati obediens non est reus homicidii, si eius inperio quemlibet flagitiosum interfecerit; si homicidas, et venenarios punire non est effusio sanguinis, sed legum ministerium; si pax ecclesiae mesticiam consolatur perditorum; si illi, qui zelo catholicae matris accensi excommunicatos interficiunt, homicidae non iudicantur: patet, quod malos non solum flagellari, sed etiam interfici licet.*

[115] C. 23, q. 5, c. 41: *Non peccat qui ex officio nocentem interficit.*

[116] C. 23, q. 5, c. 41: . . . . *cum homo iuste occiditur, lex eum occidit, non tu.*

crimes before God.[117] On the other hand, in the reproach of the evil ones God the omnipotent is pleased,[118] and enemies of the church religion also ought to be coerced by wars.[119] Gratian writes,

> It is briefly demonstrated that the good ones laudably pursue the evil ones, and evil ones damnably pursue the good. That the apostle said, "moreover who are you, that you judge another's servant?" ought to be understood regarding the hidden things of another's heart. When vengeance can be inferred, it is shown. Now it remains to show what ought to be inferred and that more esteemed are they who are punished, than those who are left unpunished, which is proved by the authority of many.[120]

---

[117] C. 23, q. 8, c. 13: *Crimina pro Deo punire non est crudelitas sed pietas.*
[118] C. 23, q. 4, c. 47: *In correptione malorum Deus omnipotens placatur.*
[119] C. 23, q. 4, c. 48: *Ecclesiasticae religionis inimici etiam bellis sunt cohercendi.*
[120] C. 23, q. 4, d.p. c. 49: *Breviter monstratum est, quod boni laudabiliter persecuntur malos, et mali dampnabiliter persecuntur bonos. Illud autem Apostoli: "Tu autem quis es, qui iudicas servum alienum?" de occultis alieni cordis intelligendum est. Quod vindicta inferri possit, monstratum est. Nunc restat ostendere, quod debet inferri, et quod magis diliguntur illi, qui puniuntur, quam qui inpuniti relinquuntur; quod utrumque multorum auctoritate probatur.*

This dictum emphasizes the beneficial effects of punishment. In fact, God is provoked to wrath when punishment is deferred.[121] Vengeance, which does well toward correction, ought not to be prohibited.[122] A Christian ought to pursue those things which are contrary to truth.[123]

Use of force in *persecutio* of heretics is not culpable, but rational and just. The church, like Jesus, has the sword. Just as Jesus expelled the merchants from the temple, the Church rightfully persecutes, and even kills, the heretics because the Church has the sword. The church ought to force the evil ones to good, just as Christ forced Paul.[124] Nor do the heretics have a legitimate claim for redress in the taking of their property. Gratian states that the heretics unjustly possess ecclesiastical property,[125] since as heretics they are cut off from the body of Christ and cannot hold a spirit of justice.[126] Therefore, catholics can lawfully take the property of heretics, who really do not lawfully possess the property in the first place:

---

[121] C. 23, q. 4, c. 50: *Ad iram Deus provocatur, cum peccata puniri differuntur.*
[122] C. 23, q. 4, c. 51: *Vindicta, que ad correctionem valet, non est prohibenda.*
[123] C. 23, q. 4, c. 52: *Que veritati contraria sunt Christianus persequi debet.*
[124] C. 23, q. 6, c. 1: *Ecclesia malos debet cogere ad bonum, sicut Christus Paulum coegit.*
[125] C. 23, q. 7, c. 3: *Res ecclesiasticae ab hereticis iniuste possidentur.*
[126] C. 23, q. 7, c. 4: *Qui a corpore Christi preciditur spiritum iusticiae tenere non potest.*

Therefore by these authorities it is shown clearly that property which are wickedly possessed by heretics, are justly snatched by catholics, nor therefore are they said to possess another's property.[127]

In contrast to Gratian's emphasis on the office of killing that alleviates the act of killing of people like those considered as heretics, Hostiensis, with his presumption against the use of force, considers the status of the victims of force. Even the enemies of God are accorded some status; clerics with temporal jurisdiction are not permitted to urge others toward snatching weapons for the defense of the oppressed and toward attacking the enemies of God:

> It is not permitted for clerics, and especially those who hold temporal jurisdiction, to urge other toward snatching weapons for defense of the oppressed, and toward attacking the enemies of God. Likewise, on behalf of own, and by defense of own fatherland or of paternal laws, and for peace, justice ought to be defended: war is not waged so that peace is acquired.[128]

---

[127] C. 23, q. 7, d.p. c. 4: *His igiture auctoritatibus liquido monstratur, quod eo, que ab hereticis male possidentur, a catholicis iuste auferuntur, nec ideo aliena possidere dicuntur.*
[128] Hostiensis, *Summa aurea*, p. 357: *Licet non clericis, et maxime qui iurisdictionem habent temporalem, hortari alios ad arripendum arma pro defensione oppressorum, et ad impugnandum inimicos Dei. Item pro sua, & patriae suae seu*

Furthermore, Hostiensis elaborates on the limitations on clerics with respect to the use of weapons, by stating the opinions of canonists on the use of certain weapons prohibited to clerics only:

> some say that clerics can use arms of defense such as the round bronze Roman shield or the breastplate, but that they cannot use arms of attack, such as sword, lance, or other sword. Others say that in inevitable necessity, only in self-defense and not in defense of others, they can take up all weapons for defending, although if they can evade, they should not take up weapons. Others say that the authority of the pope enables them to take up weapons; at another time they cannot. Gratian says that they can, not in their own person, but through others. . . . Others say. . . . that clerics can use weapons themselves.[129]

---

*legum paternarum defensione, et pace, iustitia tuenda: bellum non geritur, ut pax acquiratur.*

[129] Hostiensis, *Summa aurea*, p. 357: *In hoc etiam est dissensio. Quidam non dicunt, quod clerici possunt uti armis defensionis tamen, ut clypeo, lorica, sed non impugantionis, ut ense, lancea, aliquo gladio. Alii dicunt, quod in necessitate inevitabili pro se tantum, non pro aliis ad defendendum possunt omnia arma sumere: sed si aliter possunt evadere, non sumant. . . . Alii dicunt quod authoritate Papae haec possunt, alias non Gratianus dicit quod possunt, non in*

Hostiensis also considers the avenue of self-defense by those legitimately or not legitimately attacked. In an example in the crusades against infidels and heretics on the authority of the pope, Hostiensis adds that where "he uses the sword uses it justly, and consequently he who defends himself against such use defends himself rashly."[130] It can be inferred that where sword is *not* used justly against the victim of force, that person may justifiably defend himself. If the faithful wage war and think that the objects are unfaithful, when in fact they are not, the war does not belong to the first category ("Roman"), and the other side has the right to defend.

Although enemies refer to those who offend the Church, against whom Roman war can be waged, those who wrongly wage and do not comply to the restrictions are also considered in terms of the legitimacy of their actions. Although the first category of war describes war waged by the faithful against the unfaithful in a just war, there is always the possibility that the objects are in fact not the "unfaithful" prescribed by law. In such a case the believing warriors will be liable for the consequences of their actions, regardless of their "intent" to wage a just war against the non-believers.

---

*persona propria, sed per alios. . . . . hortando eos ad pugnam. . . . alii dicunt in dist. quod clerici possunt uti armis se. . . .*

[130] Hostiensis, *Summa aurea*, p. 359: *qui gladio utitur, iuste facit, et per consequensis, qui defendit se, temerarie se defendit.*

Hostiensis' consideration of restitution further demonstrates the limitation on the use of force. Hostiensis, again referring to his seven categories of war, states that although in Roman, judicial, licit and necessary wars, one is not responsible for restitution, in presumptuous, rash and voluntary war, anyone is responsible for restitution.[131] This categorization, concrete and detailed, makes possible instances that require restitution, as opposed to Gratian's broader concept of justified wars based on correct intent, in which case law is doing the killing, not the agent, and the agent is not personally responsible. Although on the surface Gratian and Hostiensis do not differ in principle and theory, Hostiensis' concrete and detailed categorization renders a procedural redress more possible for victims of unjust uses of force.

A comparison of Gratian's treatment of the use of force in his *Decretum* and Hostiensis' treatment of just war in his *Summa aurea* reveals a shifting notion of the defensive use of force from the legitimacy of use of force sanctioned by the church to restrictions of the use of force by imposition of a secular set of criteria. Gratian considered a legitimate use of force as that which is authorized by the church receiving divine command. The injuries that force must avenge were those committed against God, in the disruption of the peace and unity of the church and in the unjust

---

[131] Hostiensis, *Summa aurea*, p. 360: *ergo in Romano, iudiciali, licito et necessario non tenetur quis ad restutionem. In praesumptuoso vero, temerario, et voluntario tenetur quilibet ad restitutionem.*

treatment of neighbor. Furthermore, Gratian focused on the presumption of legitimacy and sacredness by adopting Augustine's notion of intent, *praeparatione cordis*, and *caritas* to protect the peace of the church at divine command. Gratian based the legitimacy of killing on intent, the nature of the office of the agent that excused personal responsibility (because it was the law that killed), and the culpability of the object, such as heretics.

On the other hand, Hostiensis focused on the secular authority in a just war and the temporal goal of recovering property and defending *patria* and paternal laws. As a result, he limited instances of force. His presentation of objective criteria (categorizations of war and characterizations of an unjust war) and restrictions on the use of force (the observation of truce and rules for restitution and clerics) further set limitations on sacred violence. While Gratian assumed the heretical status of the objects of force, Hostiensis presumed the illegitimacy of force and elevated the objects of the victims of force to a legal status.

Several factors account for the differences in the treatments of force by Gratian and Hostiensis. For one, the nature of their works dictated their discussion. Gratian was attempting to compile what became the first systematic and comprehensive textbook of canon law. He divided his work into three parts, and included numerous scriptural references and ecclesiastical prescriptions; hence, he necessarily dealt with theological issues, like predestination, which Gratian employed to emphasize his points. On the other hand Hostiensis' work is a

*Summa*; it summarized legal scholarship on various points, and retained only a few biblical citations and references.

For another, they lived in different centuries. Gratian lived in the midst of Gregorian reform, and his approach to issues involving church and secular authorities reflected the reformers' interests. Chodorow even argued that his *Decretum* was written in support of the Haimeric party. Hostiensis, on the other hand, lived at a time when both the imperial and ecclesiastical sides were determined to restore their rights and liberties. Tension between Frederick II, crowned emperor at Rome in 1220, and Pope Gregory IX was particularly acute here, as the double excommunication of Frederick by Gregory IX demonstrates. Furthermore, Hostiensis wrote after over a century of canonist activity since Gratian's masterpiece. This placed him in a position to integrate different considerations and make certain issues more concrete.

Factors such as the nature of their respective works, political contexts behind their writings, particularly reform and conflicts between pope and emperor, and the development of juristic activity in the twelfth and thirteenth centuries no doubt contributed to the differences in their approach. Nevertheless, it is these contexts that fostered the distinctive approaches of Gratian and Hostiensis whose substantive discussions on just war and force reveal the legitimating emphasis of the former and the limiting focus of the latter. The comparison of these two, then, reveals a multifaceted insight into the complex topic of the use of force in the twelfth-

and thirteenth centuries.

## Bibliography

Primary Sources

Gratian. *Decretum*, in *Corpus Iuris Canonici*, vol. 1, ed. Friedberg, Emil A. Graz: Akademische Druck- U. Verlagsanstalt, 1959.

*Henrici 'Secusia Cardinalis Hostiensis Aurea summa: Nicolae Superantii adnotationibus & quibusdam excerptis ex Summa celeberrimi Iur. Vtr. Doct. F. Martini abbatis (vt ferunt) contemporanei Azonis, & Accursij, illustrata: nunc tandem ad incorruptum authoris exemplar diligentissima restituta: cum sumarijs, & indice locupletissimis. Summa aurea.* Venetiis: Apud Iuntas, 1581.

Henry, of Segusio, Cardinal. *Summa aurea.* Henrici de Segusio; prefazione di Oreste Vighetti. Torino: Bottega d'Erasmo, 1963.


Secondary Sources

Brundage, James A. " 'Cruce Signari': The Rite for Taking the Cross in England," *Traditio* 22 (1966), 289-310.

_____. "Holy War and the Medieval Lawyers,"

in *The Holy War*, ed. Thomas Patrick Murphy. Columbus: Ohio State university Press, 1976.

_____. *Medieval Canon Law*. London and New York: Longman Group Limited, 1995.

_____. "The Hierarchy of Violence in Twelfth- and Thirteenth-Century Canonists," *International History Review* 17 (1995), 670-692.

_____. "The Limits of the War-Making Power: The Contribution of Medieval Canonists," in *The Crusades, Holy War and Canon Law*, ed. James A. Brundage. Aldershot: Variorum, 1991, XI.

Chodorow, Stanley. *Christian Political Theory and Church Politics in the Mid-Twelfth Century: The Ecclesiology of Gratian's Decretum*. Berkely: University of California Press, 1972.

Cowdrey, H. E. J. "The Genesis of the Crusades: The Springs of Western Ideas of Holy War," in *The Holy War*, ed. Thomas Patrick Murphy. Columbus: Ohio State University Press, 1976.

Gallagher, Clarence S.J. *Canon Law and the Christian Community: The Role of Law in the Church According to the Summa Aurea of Cardinal Hostiensis*. Roma: Universita

Gregoriana Editrice, 1978.

Hartigan, Richard Shelly. "Saint Augustine on War and Killing: The Problem of the Innocent," *Journal of the History of Ideas* 27 (1966), 195-204.

Hehl, Ernst-Dieter. *Kirche und Krieg im 12. Jahrhundert: Studien zu kanonischem Recht und politischer Wirklichkeit.* Stuttgart: Anton Hiersemann, 1980.

Kantorowicz, Ernst H. "*Pro Patria Mori* in Medieval Political Thought," *American Historical Review* 56 (1951), 472-492.

Muldoon, James. "Extra Ecclesiam non est Imperium: The Canonists and the Legitimacy of Secular Power." *Studia Gratiana* 9 (1966), 553-580.

_____. "The Remonstrance of the Irish Princes and the Canon Law Tradition of the Just War," *American Journal of Legal History* 22 (1978), 309-325.

Pennington, Kenneth. "The Rite for Taking the Cross in the Twelfth Century," *Traditio* 30 (1974), 429-443.

_____. "*The Just War in the Middle Ages*," *Canadian Journal of History* 11 (1976), 367-370.

Pick, Lucy K. "*Signaculum Caritatis et Fortitudinis*: Blessing the Crusader's Cross in France," *Revue Benedictine* 105: 3-4 (1995), 381-416.

*Revised Medieval Latin Word-List from British and Irish Sources*, prepared by R. E. Latham. London: The Oxford University Press, 1965, pp. 188-189.

Russell, Frederick H. "Innocent IV's Proposal to Limit Warfare," *Proceedings of the Fourth International Congress of Medieval Canon Law*, ed. Stephan Kuttner. *Monumenta Iuris Canonici*, Ser. C: Subsidia, vol. 5. Citta del Vaticano: Biblioteca Apostolica Vaticana, 1976, 383-399.

_____. "*Kirche und Krieg im 12. Jahrhundert: Studien zu kanonischem Recht und politischer Wirklichkeit*," *Speculum* 57 (1982), 618-621.

_____. "Love and Hate in Medieval Warfare: The Contribution of Saint Augustine," *Nottingham Medieval Studies* 31 (1987), 108-124.

_____. "Only Something Good Can Be Evil": The Genesis of Augustine's Secular Ambivalence," *Theological Studies* 51 (1990), 698-716.

_____. *The Just War in the Middle Ages.* Cambridge: Cambridge University Press, 1975.

# Understanding "Intent" in Criminal Law via Gratian's *Decretum* and St. Augustine

Intent is a significant element in the determination of a criminal conduct in current Western jurisprudence. Mere action of commission or omission would normally not constitute a criminal offense. The concept of intention encompasses various degrees and descriptions of human volition behind manifest acts: willful, reckless, purposeful, in-tentional. Intent is a concept that owes much of its profundity and multi-dimensional character to the intellectual and legal developments of the twelfth- and thirteenth-century Western world.

During this time, canon law underwent a legal renaissance and reached a height in its articulations. In the 1140s, Master Gratian compiled the first systematic and comprehensive collection of ecclesiastical laws and prescriptions, which Gratian analyzed and harmonized through legal reasoning. Gratian dealt with contemporary concerns of church governance and religious conduct. The product, Gratian's *Decretum*, sparked subsequent intense debates and analyses among canon lawyers who continued to dissect, reformulate, and contribute to the different ramifications of church doctrines and moral principles.

Underneath the more tangible concerns of the conduct of Christian people in the *Decretum* was a focus on the role of human intent. In *Causa* 23 of the *Decretum*, for instance, legal reasoning based on intention dictated Gratian's reconciling of contradictory positions on the use of force. Through a focus on intent, such as the disposition of the heart (*non tam ostentatione corporis quam preparatione cordis*),[132] Gratian argued that certain uses of force and violence were conclusively legitimate, despite contradictory positions in church tradition regarding the matter of force, war *vindicta* and death penalty.

Gratian's use of *preparatione cordis* both indicates the intellectual atmosphere of the twelfth century and reflects upon St. Augustine's formulation in the fourth and fifth centuries. Gratian's use of the phrase comes directly from Augustine's writings,[133]

---

[132] C. 23, q. 1, dict. post c. 1 and C. 23, q. 1, dict. post c. 7.
[133] C. 23, q. 1, c. 2: ". . . . Denique ista precepta magis sunt ad **preparationem cordis**, quam ad opus, quod in aperto fit, ut teneatur in secreto animi patiencia cum benivolentia, in manifesto autem id fiat, quod eis videtur prodesse, quibus bene velle

and Gratian's main source in discussing the will of an actor is Augustine. Gratian cites Augustine's sermon on the son of the centurion to point out that *precepta patienciae virtute animi, non ostentatione corporis servanda sunt.* [134] Gratian also quotes Augustine's letter to Boniface (epistle CCVII) to support his contention that *in bellicis armis multi Deo placere possunt,* if the intent and purpose of war is *ut pax acquiratur.* [135] Furthermore, Gratian refers to Augustine's writing regarding the diverse observances of the church to illustrate the principle, *pacata sunt bella, que geruntur, ut mali coherceantur et boni subleventur.* [136] Wars were legitimate when and if they were waged for necessary and good purpose. For Gratian, Augustine was a significant and authoritative source for legitimating wars waged by proper inward disposition of the heart.

    This matter of one's inward disposition, one's intention in willing to do something, is really a subset and an offshoot of the grand theological tension between human free will and God's grace. Human beings are 100 percent free to will something, while God's grace is 100 percent controlling. Hence, at the same time that

---

debemus. . . . " (boldprint mine).
[134] C. 23, q. 1, c. 2.
[135] C. 23, q. 1, c. 3.
[136] C. 23, q. 2, c. 6.

God is not the source of human foibles, He is nevertheless in control over both the course and the outcome of events, including the determination of eternal salvation for some and damnable punishment for others. It is a paradox that defies human reasoning and logic, but one that Augustine was not reluctant to defend and attempt to articulate.

Augustine's preoccupation of man's free will and God's grace is evident throughout his voluminous writings, expressed or implied, in various contexts. Augustine's formulations had a tremendous impact on subsequent generations, primarily because the breadth of his written material afforded him an authoritative status. In certain points in medieval history, such as the fifth, ninth and twelfth centuries, various theologians and thinkers attempted to interpret and challenge what they saw as Augustine's presentation of the dilemma. In this way, Augustine became a significant elaborator and articulator of the concept of intention in light of human responsibility in the free choice of the will.

What exactly did Augustine say? How did he present and then explain the tension between grace and free will? How can that be interpreted? In what context did he present his arguments? Such inquiries are basic to understanding just how subsequent generations understood Augustine and what was the nature of Augustine's "influence." More specifically, Augustine's approach to the dilemma warrants a scrutiny of Augustine on Paul.

In light of the broad scheme introduced above, this paper will seek to understand Augustine's arguments against Pelagians in some of his treatises, especially the one on grace and free will, and Augustine's usage of Paul's epistle to Romans in these writings. This letter to Romans contains a dynamic presentation of the theology of divine grace and human responsibility. Augustine's approach to the dilemma involved his reliance on Romans for a careful balancing of two doctrines of grace and free will (in their different ramifications) and an ultimate resignation in God's infinite wisdom.

In Romans, Paul posits free choice of will of man and God's grace and predestination. It is difficult to read and understand Paul's discussion of free will without simultaneously considering God's grace. From chapters 1-11, Paul presents a theological treatise, juxtaposing man's responsibility and God's sovereignty that entails his grace. God's dominance is evident through-out: from the beginning that presents God's predestination of Paul to God's working for the good of His people (8:28), irresistible will that is entirely indisputable and fair in administration (chapter 9), and irrevocability of God's gifts (11:29). At the same time, man has free choice to obey or disobey and so are without excuse (chapter one). In the remaining chapters (12-16), Paul comments on the practical application that follows the theological premise: God's sovereignty (predestination, mercy), rather than an excuse for evil or indifference, becomes the framework within which man should strive to do what God wants. The beginning of part two of Romans begins with this thought: in view of God's mercy discussed in the prior chapters, which involved God's election, Paul urges the readers to live holy lives pleasing to God (12:1).

Paul's letter presents the ramification of the dynamic in concrete ways. On the one hand, men have choice to suppress the truth (1:18), become fools and choose not to glorify God (1:21), invent ways of doing evil and disobey their parents (1:30), and continue to do things that deserve death (1:32). People have choice to count themselves dead to sin and alive to God (6:11), to refuse sin (6:12) and offer themselves to God (6:13). Their freedom to choose makes them responsible for their actions; they have no excuse. On the other hand, God is in control and it is up to God to decide who will be saved or not in the first place. God sets people apart (1:1), He plans things in advance (1:2), He wills things to happen (1:10), and He gives men over to depravity so that men do what they ought not to do

(1:24, 26). He chose Jacob but rejected Esau (9:13); God's mercy determines, not man's desire or effort (9:16).

Chapter seven of Romans adds another element to the equation between God's grace and man's free choice of will. Even after man's choice to submit to God, which is the working of His grace, man still struggles with sin. Paul admits that he does not understand what he does, for what he wants to do, he does not do, but what he hates he does (7:15). Sin living in him acts (7:17), and although he has the desire to do what is good, he cannot carry it out (7:18). Paul continues: "For what I do is not the good I want to do; no the evil I do not want to do -- this I keep on doing" (7:19, NIV). When he wants to do good, evil is right there (7:21). "For in my inner being I delight in God's law; but I see another law at work. . . . making me a prisoner of the law of sin" (7:22-23, NIV). Man's free will is restricted, since sin prevents him from doing what he wants to do. This constant struggle with sin further reinforces the necessity of God's grace throughout life because of the limitation of human will.

Augustine's comments on Romans illuminate the dynamic relationship between free will and grace and a particular attention to God's grace. In his treatise "On Forgiveness of Sins and Baptism," Augustine includes a section (Chapter 43)[137] on Romans. Here, Augustine acknowledged a heavy reliance on Apostle Paul's writings, because "it fell to him to recommend the grace of God with especial earnestness, in opposition to those who gloried in their works, and who, ignorant of God's righteousness, and wishing to establish their own, submitted not to the righteousness of God" (31). Then followed various selections from Romans that to Augustine summarized Romans' position on grace: people are justified freely by His grace which entails no human merit, involves righteousness without works and delivers one from the body of death that is the battleground of the war between the law of God and law of sin (31-32).

Augustine emphasized the grace aspect of the equation because of the prevalence of Pelagian focus on free will and an undermining of grace. At the same time, Augustine in turn did not downplay the role of human responsibility in their free will, but rather placed it in its proper context. Augustine articulates this in the 215th epistle to Valentinus (439-40), in which he clarifies

---

[137] The numbers inside the parentheses refer to either the chapter numbers of particular treatises or the page numbers in *A Select Library of the Nicene and Post-Nicene Fathers of the Christian Church*, volume 5, ed. Philip Schaff (Grand Rapids: WM. B. Eerdmans Publishing Company, 1980). Other references of and quotations from English translations of Augustine's anti-Pelagian works also come from this edition.

the relationship in light of Romans 2:8-9: "The good, indeed, shall receive their reward according to the merits of their own good-will, but then they received this very good-will through the grace of God" (439). It is really all a matter of a right perspective, that does not belittle any one aspect. For instance, the soundness of the catholic faith "neither denies free will whether for an evil or a good life, nor attributes to it so much power that it can avail anything without God's grace, whether that it may be changed from evil to good, or that it may persevere in the pursuit of good, or that it may attain to eternal good when there is no further fear of failure" (439). Augustine then provides an exhortation from Romans 12:3: "not to think of yourselves more highly than you ought to think; but to think soberly, according as God hath dealt to every man the measure of faith" (439-40). He warns against turning aside to the right, by saying that one's will suffices for that person to perform good works, or to the left, where they say, "Let us do evil that good may come" (Romans 3:8). On the other hand, Augustine states the following: "do not uphold free will in such wise as to attribute good works to it without the grace of God, nor so defend and maintain grace as if, by reason of it, you may love evil works in security and safety, -- which may God's grace itself avert from you!" By restating Romans 6:1-2, Augustine further corrects the distorted understanding of those who give undue emphasis on the effect of grace on sinners: "what shall we say, then? Shall we continue in sin that grace may abound?" (440).

The Pelagian Controversy was significant with respect to Augustine's theology on grace and free will. It "thrust Augustine into the limelight;" it was a point after which his books spoke for him and effected Augustine's international reputation.[138] It was in the controversy with Pelagians that Augustine articulated his position on the matters of a human soul and salvation; sin and free will.[139]

Pelagius held the belief contrary to the theology of grace; to Pelagius, people were capable of taking action in a way to win God's favor.[140] In various writings, Augustine gave the readers a glimpse of the damnable Pelagian doctrines. In a letter to Valentinus and the monks of Adrumetum, he wrote that the Pelagian heretics "say that the grace of God is bestowed according to our own merits, so that he who glories has to glory not in the Lord, but in himself, -- that is to say, in man, not in the Lord" (437). Pelagians placed a disproportionate empha-

---

[138] James J. O'Donnell, "The Authority of Augustine," p. 5.
[139] O'Donnell, *Augustine*, p. 61.
[140] James J. O'Donnell, *Augustine*. (Boston: Twayne Publishers, 1985), p. 12.

sis on individual responsibility, or human merits.

Furthermore, in chapter 6 of "On Grace and Free Will," Augustine pointed out that the Pelagian heresy caused the heart of the adherent to depart from the Lord. The problem is not so much the terminology but the whole mindset. What Pelagius called free will was not the same concept in an Augustinian context. For Augustine, free will existed inextricably with God's grace; for the Pelagians, free will was autonomous from God's control. This was more than a matter of emphasis. In chapter 23, Augustine commented that Pelagians maintained that the law was the grace of God which helped one not to sin. For the Pelagians, man's obedience to law brought salvation. In chapter 26 Augustine further remarked that the Pelagians contended that the grace, which was neither the law nor nature, availed only to the remission of past sins, but not to the avoidance of future ones. The Pelagians emphasized the role of human beings to love and demonstrate faith.

The Pelagians placed greater emphasis on free will; their view ignored the absoluteness of God's grace, which in fact ultimately established free will. Augustine's emphasis, on the other hand, was God's grace. This was really a matter of emphasis from the human point of view, since one can only see three dimensions, while the complexity of divine truth demands additional dimensions that human beings can never see.

Against the Pelagian exclusive emphasis on free will, Augustine uses Romans to demonstrate the coexistence, compatibility and cooperation of God's grace and free will: Romans 3:6 refers to God's judging the world, which is possible because of free will of man, just as God's saving the world occurs because of His grace. He further proves the centrality of grace. Romans 9:21 supports the point that God justifies because He, in his grace, distinguishes between a vessel to honour, and not to dishonour (437). Furthermore, the existence of free will does not trump divine role in salvation. Human beings cannot attain salvation by their merits, only by God's grace.

In "On Grace and Free Will," written also to Valentinus, Augustine seeks to present a balanced version of the relationship between grace and free will. He continues to counterbalance the two sides in a manner least demeaning to either side by references to and support from Romans. He first starts with free will and uses Romans 1:18-20 to support the existence of free will in man (444). The very commandments of God, for example the command not to be overcome of evil (Romans 12:1), attests to the existence of free will (445). The passage that exhorts one not to be overcome by evil, but overcome evil with good (Romans 12:21), to Augustine, demonstrates that one has no excuse to plead from ignorance, nor reason to blame God because evil is within the person (446). Those who sin out of free will in ignorance are also without excuse as Romans 2:12 states (445).

    Romans 12:21 continues to provide Augustine with the arsenal for presenting the compatibility of man's free will and God's grace. With chapter 6, Augustine turns his attention to God's grace and uses Romans 12:21. It is a response to free will that claims mastery of concupiscence; at the same time, "in order. . . . that this victory may be gained [overcome evil with good], grace renders its help; and were not this help given, then the law would be nothing but the strength of sin. For concupiscence is increased and receives greater energies from the prohibition of the law, unless the spirit of grace helps" (447). He concludes this chapter eight with his point about the compatibility of the two, albeit in context of his emphasis on grace in the context of the Pelagian threat: "It follows, then, that the victory in which sin is vanquished is nothing else than the gift of God, who in this contest helps free will" (447). The coexistence of the two is further explicated in chapter ten: "free will and God's grace are simultaneously commended" (448).

Augustine uses Romans 4:4 to critique the Pelagians who declare that God's grace is given according to men's merits. If it were so, grace would not be grace. Those who receive according to merit do so out of debt, not grace (448). Augustine sets out to prove that grace is not given according to men's merits but itself makes all good desert (448-9). The victory that makes us conquerors (Romans 8:37) is accomplished not by ourselves but by God, since Romans 9:16 makes clear that it is not of man who wills and tries, but of God that shows mercy (449). Works determine what God renders someone (Romans 2:6), because works proceed from faith which justifies a man (451).

The relationship between free will (for example to obey law) and grace is connected to that between works and faith, as Augustine's discussion in chapters 18 and following (451ff) demonstrates. Just as by free will one cannot attain salvation, a person is justified by faith, not by works (Romans 3:28). God's grace is the source of faith, good works, justification and eternal life(Romans 6:23) (451-453). The explication and a satisfying resolution of the tension between free will and grace involves the profound issue of salvation-- by faith as opposed to by works and obedience to law. Those who are not led by the spirit of God and with the help of the grace of God are ignorant of God's righteousness and seek to establish their own (Romans 10:3). Free will is inadequate because it will never bring salvation to anyone, since neither law nor nature is grace that leads to one's status as a Christian (454).

Augustine corrects Pelagius' claim that law is the grace of God that aids one not to sin. This position, according to Augustine, contradicts Paul, since while the law works toward conviction of sin (leading to salvation) law itself kills. Augustine quotes Romans 8:12-13 to support this: by mortifying the deeds of the body (equal to the letter, the law), one shall live. Free will is something that can be guided and Augustine uses the above passage to deter the free will from pursuing evil and to doing good. One ought rather be led by the Spirit of God as sons of God (Romans 8:14). Sin has no dominion over one who is under grace, not under law (Romans 6:4).

Augustine gives more emphasis on grace. Human beings are also insufficient in terms of their will and hence need God's assistance. This is the reason for praying to God (457). Whether it be love for God and neighbor or faith in God, God's grace is the source, not human will (460-61). Augustine emphasizes what grace can do: effects of the fulfillment of the law, the deliverance of nature, and the suppression of sin's dominion (455). Even the ability to believe is not one's own doing but from God who deals with men according to the proportion of faith (Romans 12:3). It is "the spirit of grace" that "causes us to have faith, in order that through faith we may, on praying for it, obtain the ability to do what we are commanded." Augustine further uses Romans 10:14 to point out that even calling on God is preceded by His grace.

On the balance of things, Augustine points out that Paul "constantly puts faith before the law; since we are not able to do what the law commands unless we obtain the strength to do it by the prayer of faith" (455). God trumps our free will because He can convert obstinate wills of men (455), even if we do not deserve His grace. Both free will and grace play a role in heart's conversion (456). Will is initially prepared by the Lord (Proverbs 8:35), and the purpose for asking Him is that "it is he who makes us act, by applying efficacious powers to our will" (457). The great will to love, which in Romans 13:8-10 fulfills the law is prompted by God. God's cooperation in Romans 8:28 is further quoted by Augustine in Chapter 33 (457-58). Love comes from God (459), and we love God because He loved us first and we choose Him only because He first chose us (459-60). This love from God, mentioned in Romans 5:3,4,5, enables us to endure hardship with patience (460).

Such grace of God guides and controls the wills of men. As Romans 9:22 states, some are vessels of wrath fitted to destruction (461). God does whatsoever he wishes in the hearts of even wicked men -- he gives them up to uncleanness (Romans 1:23), to vile affections (Romans 1:26) and reprobate mind (Romans 1:28) (462). God operates on men's hearts to incline their wills "whithersoever he pleases" (463). This gratuitous grace is exemplified in infants.

Augustine casts the relationship between free will and grace, not in opposition, but as descriptions of different aspects of divine will, use and purpose. One talks about "free will" to reveal the responsibility of human individuals, but one must confine to that arena, and not use free will to undermine divine dominion in every area of life, including in the matter of salvation. Human beings have free will and have no excuse for their actions (they cannot blame ignorance, for instance); yet, this does not make God a mere being in the background. In fact, God plans everything in such a way that a certain man may reject, while another one may not, yet this neither absolves human beings of their responsibility or puts blame on God for unfairness. To cast it in this way is inherently flawed because God's fairness and justice is an irrefutable premise, which man in arrogance might attack, but their premise is flawed.

Because of the limitation of human

language, understanding and perception, the best solution ultimately is to resign in God's infinite wisdom. As Isaiah had declared, human thoughts are not God's, neither are man's ways God's (Isaiah 55), and as Apostle Paul confessed, God's foolishness is still wiser than man's wisdom (I Corinthians 1:25). Augustine himself is conscious of the limited nature of language to perfectly convey divine truths: "it is, however, to be feared lest all these and similar testimonies of Holy Scripture (and undoubtedly there are a great many of them), in the maintenance of free will, be understood in such a way as to leave no room for God's assistance and grace in leading a godly life and a good conversation, to which the eternal reward is due" (446). There is an indispensable need for balance, wisdom, and right mindset, a heart that does not depart from the Lord. One needs to avoid the mistake of the three friends of Job, who spoke some beautiful language of theology, but who evidently missed the mark in speaking of God what is right as Job had (Job 42:8).

Augustine uses Romans 11:33 to emphasize the depth of the riches of the wisdom and knowledge of God, although "perverse men, who do not reflect upon these unsearchable judgments and untraceable ways, indeed, but are ever prone to censure, being unable to understand, have supposed the apostle to say, and censoriously gloried over him for saying, "Let us do evil, that good may come!" Such logic was inherently flawed: "their language, therefore, ought not to be: "Let us do evil, that good may come;" but: "We have done evil, and good has come; let us henceforth do good, that in the future world we may receive good for good, who in the present life are receiving good for evil" (463-64). The reason why one is shown grace while another is not-- must be explained with reference to the secret judgments of God-- a sense of "resignation" of faith was required (464). Augustine ends his treatise on grace and free will on this note of resignation: understanding and wisdom must be sought from God (465).

In other treatises in defense of faith against the Pelagians, Augustine's comments in light of his use of Romans further reinforce Augustine's priority of grace over free will (since the theology of grace sets the whole scheme in the first place) and a sense of resignation in the face of human limitations. For example, Augustine's comments on Romans 9:16 is insightful. The verse states that "it is not of him that willeth, nor of him that runneth, but of God that showeth mercy." God's grace dominates, whether it be in our doing good, avoiding sin, putting in hard work, or being righteous -- all those acts of "free will" are done by the grace of God which is the irrefutable premise. Augustine constantly focuses on rewards that are given to the unworthy, and hence equals grace (199). Paul's finishing his course (I Corinthians 4:7) is the result of God's mercy as explicated in Romans 9:16. Even Paul credits God's grace behind all his labors, and man abstains from sin because of God's grace (200).

Not only is grace predominant, Augustine acknowledges the limitation of language. He remarks that on Romans 9:16 itself, "no safe conclusion, therefore, can be drawn." Pelagius' exposition that the apostle must not be regarded as entertaining the sentiment, but rather as refuting it is "perverse" (200-201). To Augustine, Pelagius is considering free will as the source of man's actions, not as means by which God's grace is administered, and that "whomsoever God deigns he calls and whom he wills he makes religious." Pelagius attributed to free will what should rightly be attributed to God's doing (234) .

Romans 9:16 is a reference point for Augustine's discussion of Pelagian confusion of fate and grace. Pelagius thinks that where God's grace is not given in respect of our merits but according to His own most merciful will, such is fate. Augustine changes the presentation of the argument: if one were to forsake God's grace because it was "fatalistic," one would be left with admitting that by man's merits one attains God's grace, which is clearly contradicted by Paul (395). Augustine further notes the difference between grace and fate by giving an example from baptism. Infants receive baptism regardless of their merits. An infant born of Christ's foes could be baptized in Christ by the mercy of Christians while the infant of religious people could be forestalled by death before it can be washed in the laver of regeneration. According to Augustine, the Pelagians cling to a simplistic model that gives possibilities of only merit and fate. However, both merit and fate may not exist(as seen in the example of the baptism of infants), and it is the grace that God gives freely by which even the wicked are justified (395-96). This grace of God, as opposed to fate, stands above all the stars, heavens, and angels: "In a word, the assertors of fate attribute both men's good and evil doings and fortunes to fate; but God in the ill fortunes of men follows up their merits with due retribution, while good fortunes He bestows by undeserved grace with a merciful will; doing both the one and the other not according to a temporal conjunction of stars, but according to the eternal and high counsel of His severity and goodness" (396).

  This acceptance of the inscrutability of God's wisdom and his justice is the ultimate explanation of grace and free will: "mercy is past finding out by which He has mercy on whom He will, no merits of his own preceding; and the truth is unsearchable by which He hardeneth whom He will. . . . For is there unrighteousness with God? Away with the thought! but His ways are past finding out. Therefore let us believe in His mercy in the case of those who are delivered, and in His truth in the case of those who are punished, without any hesitation; and let us not endeavour to look into that which is inscrutable, nor to trace that which cannot be found out" (535).

The existence of grace that seems to limit the activity of free will does not absolve people of their responsibility. The limitation exists in so far as free will is emphasized to the exclusion, or belittling, of the role of God's grace. People are responsible for their actions because their actions result from a certain frame of mind. Hence, we can talk about a person's intention and the significant role it plays in determining the legitimacy of conduct or degrees of culpability.

And largely, it is a matter of emphasis. In the limited arena of human understanding, which is partial at best, perfect compatibility of two divine concepts is impossible. Believers know that both exist, regardless of their inability to explain it (or completely understand it) through the medium of limited human language. What they can do is to defend an aspect of the ramifications of their coexistence and co-operation, although in the process they may run the risk of casting a less than satisfactory light on clarifying another aspect of the equation.

Studying Augustine through the lens of a particular treatise on free will and grace against Pelagians both reinforces this limitation of human articulation and comprehensibility, as well as the negative effects of language-- the equivocation of words. All utterances have "side effects." By articulating a particular point, certain facets may not be mentioned or reconciled with the whole system. By emphasizing one thing, another factor may be overlooked or slighted. By defending against certain people, one may feel the need to emphasize one aspect, at the expense of another, although not for the purpose of limiting the value or importance of that other side.

To talk about the "influence" of Augustine, one cannot ignore the validity or factor of the changes in the contexts and mediums. Circumstances differ and change, and so do the way people speak, express and articulate. At the time of Augustine, he felt an urgent need to protect the faith of the church, the purity of doctrines from Donatists, Pelagians, and other heretics. At the time of Gratian, the church had a pressing need to protect the ecclesiastical authorities against heretics and infidels. While the emphasis of Augustine was grace amid the Pelagian position, the latter period's emphasis was individual responsibility, against the clerical abuses and reform atmosphere.

When Gratian quotes Augustine in his arguments regarding another paradox (war, force and vengeance versus commandment to love, refrain from vengeance), Gratian uses Augustine to support what to Gratian, the product of many centuries since Augustine, see as the correct ecclesiastical position to take. When Gratian quotes Augustine in support of war, that does not necessarily mean Augustine was in support of force. We can never know what Augustine would have said, because he himself did not live at the time, place and atmosphere of Gratian's world. But, even if Augustine of Gratian is not necessarily the Augustine of the fourth- and fifth- centuries, one cannot deny the influence of Augustine throughout the centuries and down to the current Western jurisprudence-- by the sheer fact of his prominence in the debate and discourse -- be it through the selectivity, subjectivity, and prejudices of agents along the way who chose to emphasize some aspects over others.

# Bibliography

Primary Sources

*Biblia latina cum glossa ordinaria: facsimile reprint of editio princeps Adolph Rusch of Strassburg 1480-81*, introduction by Karlfries Froehlich and Margaret T. Gibson. Turnhout (Belgium): Brepols, 1992.

Gratian, *Decretum* in *Corpus Iuris Canonici*, vol. 1, ed. Emil Friedberg. Graz: Akademische Druck- u. Verlagsanstalt, 1959.

Schaff, Philip, ed. *A Select Library of the Nicene and Post-Nicene Fathers of the Christian Church*. vol. 5 Saint Augustin: Anti-Pelagian Writings. Grand Rapids: WM. B. Eerdmans Publishing Company, 1980.


Secondary Sources

Berrouard, Marie-Francois. "L'exegese augustinienne de Rom., 7, 7-25 entre 396 et 418" *Recherches Augustiniennes* 16 (1981), 101-195.

Dihle, Albrecht. *Theory of Will in Classical Antiquity*. Berkeley: University of California Press, 1992.

Klingshirn, William E. *Caesarius of Arles: The Making of a Christian Community*. Cambridge: Cambridge University Press, 1994.

Matter, E. Ann. "The Church Fathers and the *Glossa ordinaria*," *The Reception of the Church Fathers in the West: From the Carolingians to the Maurists*, vol. 1 ed. Irena Backus. Leiden (NY, Koeln): E. J. Brill, 1997.

O'Donnell, James J. *Augustine*. Boston: Twayne Publishers, 1985.

_____. "The Authority of Augustine."

Pelikan, Jaroslav. *The Emergence of the Catholic Tradition (100-600)*. Chicago: University of Chicago Press, 1971.

_____. *The Growth of Medieval Theology (600-1300)*. Chicago: University of Chicago Press, 1978.

Rist, John M. *Augustine: Ancient Thought Baptized*. Cambridge: Cambridge

University Press, 1994.

_____. "Augustine on Free Will and Predestination," *Journal of Theological Studies* 20 (1969b), 420-447.

## MEDIEVAL CANON LAW AND SACRAMENTAL THEOLOGY: THE CASE OF BAPTISM

The history of medieval canon law entails consideration of many different sources and disciplines. Legal principles from Roman law, conciliar decisions in various parts of Europe since the Late Antiquity, penitential practices embodied in Carolingian handbooks, and papal decisions in the High Middle Ages all contributed to the interworkings of medieval canon law.

Still another area is worthy of mention in light of the development of medieval canon law: theology. Until the twelfth century, it is difficult to segregate "theological" treatments as opposed to a canonical and a legal one. However, with the flowering of the legal renaissance from the twelfth century, especially with the compilation of Gratian's *Concordia Discordantium Canonum* and the legal activity it triggered, canon law acquired an identity increasingly defined and distinct.

Nowhere is this phenomenon more noticeable than in canon law's consideration of sacramental theology, especially in the sacrament of baptism. This sacrament is considered first by Lombard; it has always been included among the sacraments. It was vital, since it was considered necessary for salvation. This sacrament involved theological issues, or doctrines about God and man's status in relationship to God. Doctrines of original and actual sins, remission of sin, obtaining of salvation, eternal life, doctrine of the Trinity, and the unity of believers, are all embodied in this sacrament. On the other hand, it was of particular concern to ecclesiastical lawyers, since it determined the status of a person within the church.

Observing Gratian's consideration of the sacrament of baptism in the third section of his *Decretum, de consecr.* d. 4, cc. 1-156, and comparing it to Lombard's *Sententiae* 4. d. 2-6,[141] I plan to show the ways their

---

[141] Unless further clarity is necessary, quotations from these sources will be brief and limited to the citation of canons in Gratian's "text" on baptism (*de consec.* d. 4, cc. 1-156 (1361-1412) and *capitulae* (and subsections if necessary) in Lombard's "text" (*Sent.* 4. d.2- d.6, 2:239-276). Consequently, quotation from Gratian's text will be cited with the number of the canon followed by "c," and quotation from Lombard's text will be cited with the numbers of the *distinctio* and *capitula* followed by a "d" and "c." Gratian's headings preceding the sources he quotes as well as the canons themselves will be referred to by the number of the canons. Gratian's assertion before the cited canons or his dictum

differences of approach led to illuminate different aspects regarding baptism.

While Gratian's text is canonical and legal, his interest in theology is great. Hence, he places much emphasis on the substantial doctrine of the Trinity in his discussion on baptism. Furthermore, in his efforts to harmonize the conflicting sources, he utilizes the technique of proposing rules and exceptions to those rules. Sources that contradict the rules he asserts support the exceptional cases. As a result, he diminishes the role of personal faith when he provides exceptions with the case of infants and the mentally deficient.

On the other hand, Lombard the "theologian" is concerned with factors that contribute to the validity of the sacrament. Consequently, he utilizes a scholastic method of argumentation to focus on words and language and focuses on those texts that best support his thesis. His approach to the significance of the doctrine of Trinity in its many manifestations in baptism is less doctrinal than it is formalistic; he pays closer attention to the *way* the Trinitarian formula is validly invoked. Furthermore, rather than providing rules and exceptions to

---

following the canons, however, will be quoted in italics, as they appear in Friedberg's edition. Lombard's text comes from the second book, third edition by Collegii S. Bonaventurae Ad Claras Aquas, Grottaferrata (Romae), 1981.

explain contradictory views regarding the element of faith, he provides a more complex scheme of the distinction between *res* and sacrament in order to give a more clear direction for understanding the absolute role of faith in baptism, regardless of the cases of infants.

These issues of Trinity and faith have been common areas of discrepancy. Although the need to invoke the Trinitarian formula as the verbal aspect of baptism was a consensus, there were doubts regarding whether all three persons must be explicitly invoked. Was the baptism in Christ's name sufficient? Furthermore, faith was a necessary element of effective baptism, but what about those who, because of age or mental deficiency, were incapable of professing their faith?

With respect to these considerations of the Trinity and faith, the differences between Gratian and Lombard arise not from their conclusion but in their fine distinctions and methods of approach. In terms of structure, Lombard's organization is much more systematic. He presents his discussion in five *distinctiones*, subdivided by chapters and sections, and held together by his analyses. On the other hand, Gratian's discussion is a collection of 156 canons, with no apparent organizational principle.

However, Gratian's discussion has a structure of its own. He shapes his discussion by formulating principles before introducing the individual canons. He arranges these assertions and their supporting authorities to formulate his resolution of various issues in the form of the general rule and exceptions to that standard, which conflicting sources prove. Overall, the doctrinal substance of the Trinity and its requisite role in the baptism administered in the name of Christ is a main criterion for an effective baptism in Gratian's format of discourse. Christ is the second person of the Trinity who specifically administers the baptism in which the baptized acknowledge and believe in the whole Trinity. Both are required and not mutually exclusive, since the two serve different functions in baptism. Christ administers the baptism, and the nature of the baptism is in the nature of the Trinity.

Gratian begins by discussing the necessity of visible sacrament and invisible faith for salvation.[142] He presents the reasons in the following canons: in baptism concupiscence is extinguished,[143] and all human beings inherit original sin upon their conception.[144] Baptism, in place of circum-

---

[142] C. 1: *Sine sacramento visibili et fide invisibili nemo salvatur.*

[143] C. 2: *In baptismate concupiscentia exstinguitur, non ut non sit, sed ut non obsit.*

[144] Cc. 3-4: *Qui ex viro et muliere concipitur, cum originali peccato nascitur, nec sine baptismate salvatur.*

cision, now remits original sin and sins in general.[145] Within first several titles, Gratian has outlined the necessity, relevance and history of the sacrament.

Gratian next logically focuses on the elements necessary for a valid baptism. First, profession of faith was necessary.[146] In the case of infant, however, faith of those presenting the infant is sufficient.[147] Gratian elaborates on the very first point he made in c. 1. Baptism and faith are both necessary for salvation, but he qualifies the necessity of faith in the administration of baptism in an exceptional case. Another requisite element is the water of baptism that makes the earthly man a heavenly man.[148] In order for the water to purify sin, however, this water must be that which is sanctified by the touching of the body of the Lord.[149] Hence John's baptism, only with water and without the Holy Spirit, was not adequate, and Christ's baptism was necessary.[150] Christ

---

[145] C. 5: *Sicut nunc in baptismate, ita olim in circumcisione remittebantur peccata*; c. 6: *Originale peccatum nunc in baptismate, olim in circumcisione remittebatur.*
[146] C. 8: *Per fidem et baptisma iustificamur a peccatis.*
[147] C. 7: *Parvulis in fide offerentium prodest fides.*
[148] C. 9: *Per aquam baptismi de terreno fit homo celestis.*
[149] C. 10: *Aqua baptismi non purgaret peccata, nisi tactu dominici corporis esset sanctificata.*
[150] Christ himself was baptized in water by John the Baptist. On the inadequacy of John's Baptist's baptism for remission of sin, Gratian, near the end of

and the Holy Spirit, members of the Trinity, comprise a central place in the baptismal rite

After presenting the core elements, Gratian's discussion moves to the administration of baptism. In canons 11-18, Gratian considers the times when baptism is to be observed. Gratian lays out the rule that the baptism should occur on the two traditionally designated days of Easter and Pentecost. The former celebrates the resurrection of Christ, and the latter commemorates the descending of the Holy Spirit upon the believers. He provides an exception to the rule, when *necessitate cogente*,[151] but otherwise, no one presumes to baptize other than on those days.[152]

Gratian introduces another presumptive rule with respect to the administration of baptism. As a general rule, only a priest should presume to baptize.[153] However, Gratian provides for exceptions to this rule, namely when *necessitate cogente*.[154] Then, a woman,[155] a layman,[156] or a pagan[157] could baptize, although generally they could not.

---

the discussion, explicitly asserts that *In baptismo Iohannis non errat peccati remissio* (c. 135).
[151] C. 16.
[152] Cc. 17-18: *Nisi necessitate cogente preter Pasca et Pentecostem nullus baptizare presumat.*
[153] C. 19: *Nemo nisi sacerdos baptizare presumat.*
[154] Cc. 20-22.
[155] C. 20.
[156] Cc. 21-22.
[157] Cc. 23-24.

Baptism is equally administered whether by the good ministers or the bad ones,[158] since rather than the merits of the ministers, it is the virtue of Christ that operates in baptism.[159] As with the previous rule regarding the designated days for the administration of baptism, this rule is premised on the centrality of Christ, as a part of Trinity, in the sacrament of baptism.

This principle is also predominant throughout Gratian's discussion. In a valid baptism, Christ is the real administrator. The person performing the baptism is a mere "agent" whose status is largely irrelevant. Rather, baptism in the name of the Lord. is a proof of valid baptism.[160] This is essentially the same as saying that the necessary and sufficient component for a valid baptism that does not require a rebaptism is that which is performed in the name of Trinity.[161] Hence, a non-baptized or a heretic could effectively administer baptism, as long as the name of the Trinity is used.[162]

---

[158] C. 25: *Sicut per bonum, ita per malum ministrum eque baptisma ministratur.*
[159] Cc. 26-27: *Non merita ministrorum, sed virtus Christi in baptismate operatur.*
[160] C. 30: *Baptizantur qui tantum in nomine Domini baptizati probantur.*
[161] Cc. 28-29: *Non reiteratur baptisma, quod in nomine S. Trinitatis prestatur.*
[162] C. 31: *An approbetur baptisma, quod a non baptizato prestatur*; c. 32: *Non reiteratur baptisma, quod in fide sanctae Trinitatis ab hereticis prestatur.*

Regardless of the agent, and regardless of the absence of personal faith in certain cases, baptism is adequate, and necessary, for salvation.[163] In a rare case, shedding of blood can fulfill the function of baptism itself;[164] however, Gratian does not discuss this exceptional situation in detail. His focus lies with the general necessity of baptism, whose validity is not undermined by lay ministers.[165] Baptism is necessary for salvation even for a catechuman who lives uprightly,[166] and it is not to be repeated, as long as the elements comprising a valid baptism are there regardless of agents.[167] Even people like schismatics do not extinguish baptism nor the power of the one to be baptized.[168] Gratian reiterates the point made earlier in cc. 25-26 that when evil ones administer baptism, it is not by their power but by virtue of Christ.[169] Again and again, Gratian reiterates this point: as long as the real administrator is Jesus Christ, in whose name the human agents minister, the status

---

[163] C. 33: *Valet ad salutem baptisma, etsi non ea fide parvuli offeruntur*; cf. c. 7.
[164] C. 34: *Effusio sanguinis inplet vicem baptismi.*
[165] C. 36: *Valet baptisma, etsi per laicos ministretur.*
[166] C. 37: *Quamvis recte vivat catecuminus, sine baptismo tamen non potest salvari.*
[167] C 39: *Et per bonos et per malos ministros eque baptizat Christus.*
[168] C. 40: *Nec baptisma, nec baptizandi potestatem scismatici amittunt.*
[169] C. 41: *Mali non sua potestate, sed Christi virtute baptisma ministrant.*

of these human agents are irrelevant. As long as Christ's baptism is performed in the name of the Trinity, even heretics can administer the sacrament received in the church.[170]

As long as the Trinity is there, other matters are only extraneous. Although there are heresies and sacrilege of heretics that are clearly not sacraments,[171] when the sacraments of church are performed, they are one and the same whether performed by the good or the bad people.[172] Hence, no rebaptism should occur even after baptism by heretics,[173] and baptism by pagans in the name of the Trinity is a valid one.[174] After discussion of other issues, for example exorcism and demons, Gratian pinpoints the fact that the presence of the Trinity consecrates the font of baptism,[175] and even words of error produced by ignorance, do not impede the water of sanctification.[176]

---

[170] C. 44: *Quomodo recipiantur in ecclesia qui in nomine Trinitas apud hereticos baptizantur.*

[171] Cc. 46-48: *Heresis et sacrilegium hereticorum sunt, non sacramenta.*

[172] C. 49: *Quod bonis et malis sacramenta ecclesiae conmunia sunt.*

[173] C. 51: *Non est rebaptizandus qui ab hereticis baptizatur.*

[174] C. 52: *Baptizati a paganis in nomine baptizentur Trinitatis.*

[175] C. 71: *Quomodo fontem baptismi Trinitatis presentia consecrat.*

[176] C. 72: *Verba erroris per inpericiam prolata non inpediunt aquae sanctificationem.*

After further exploring of the implications of the Trinity at the font of baptism, including immersions, Gratian reiterates the point that even the misstatement of the Latin in the invocation of the Trinity as a result of the ignorance of the priest does not invalidate a baptism, as long as the misstatement was a result of the ignorance and not heretical tendencies.[177]

Gratian expands on the implications of the Trinity in the interval between c. 72 and c. 86, by putting less emphasis on the act of faith and more on the object of faith, Trinity, in baptism. He starts by inquiring about the mysteries celebrated at the font of baptism,[178] and includes a statement of faith in the Trinity from the canons.[179] Although the ones to be baptized must profess their

---

[177] C. 86: *De sacerdote, qui per inpericiam linguae latinae in invocatione Trinitatis deliquit.* The canon from Pope Zacharias includes the following: ". . . . si ille, qui baptizavit, non errorem introducens aut heresim, sed pro sola ignorantia Romanae locutionis infringendo linguam, ut supra diximus, hoc baptizans dixisset, non possumus consentire, ut denuo baptizentur."

[178] C. 73: *Quid significent misteria, que in fonte baptismatis celebrantur.*

[179] C. 73: ". . . . interrogavimus: Credis in Deum Patrem omnipotentem? Respondistis: Credo. Rursum interrogavimus: Credis et in Iesus Christum filium eius, qui natus est de Spiritu sancto et Maria Virgine? Respondistis singuli: Credo. Item interrogavimus: et in Spiritum sanctum? Respondistis similiter: Credo. . . ."

faith, infants are baptized by the faith of others,[180] as is the case with the sick, the mute, and the deaf.[181] With the case of the infant, it is the sacrament of faith, not the faith itself, that makes the infant faithful.[182] Nevertheless, these cases are only exceptions, and profession of another does not fare well for those who could respond on their own.[183]

Then Gratian focuses on the discussion of the number of immersions in Christian baptism. He states with the rule (thrice immersion) and asks why this is so.[184] He acknowledges the practice of once immer-sion,[185] but parallels the invocation of Trinity with thrice immersion.[186] Effective baptism is one that invokes the Trinitarian name;[187] and once immersion is

---

[180] C. 74: *Aliorum fide et professione parvuli baptizantur.*

[181] C. 74: ". . . . sicut etiam egri, muti, et surdi, quorum vice alius profitetur, ut pro eis respondeat, dum baptizantur." Also, in c. 75, Gratian asserts: *Aliorum testimoni egrotantes sunt baptizandi.*

[182] C. 76: *Sacramentum fidei, non ipsa fides parvulum facit fidelem.*

[183] C. 77: *Alterius professio non valet ei, qui per se respondere potest.*

[184] C. 78: *Quare trina mersio in baptismate celebretur.*

[185] Cc. 79-81: *De his, qui semel, non tertio in baptismate merguntur*; C. 82: *De his, qui in Christi nomine semel tantum merguntur.*

[186] C. 83: *In invocatione Trinitatis tertio in baptismate mergere debemus.*

[187] C. 84: *Rebaptizentur qui in nomine Trinitatis*

permitted.[188]

After considering other substantive issues related to baptism in cc. 87-130, such as issues of annointment, Gratian uses the last 26 canons to focus on the main points reiterated at the beginning. He wraps up his discussion of baptism by focusing on the significance of baptism. First, infants must be baptized in order to have salvation.[189] With infants, baptism is also exceptionally effective despite the fact that infants cannot profess faith themselves, since the faith of the offerors makes the infants faithful.[190]

The second effect of baptism is that the baptized attain a new status. They die to sin,[191] since it provides for remission of sin in contrast to the baptism of John,[192] which means that not only original but also actual sins are remitted.[193] Whoever is born in concupiscence is regenerated through

---

*baptizati non fuerint.*
[188] C. 85: *Semel in baptismate mergere licet.*
[189] C. 132: *Quare sit baptizandus qui de baptizato nascitur*; c. 142: *Preter baptisma Christi parvulis nulla salus promittitur.*
[190] Cc. 138-139: *Offerentium fides parvulos facit fideles.* Cf. c. 7, c. 33.
[191] C. 133: *In baptismate omnia peccata moriuntur.* C. 134: *Sicut nulli baptisma negatur, ita nemo est, qui non peccato moriatur.*
[192] C. 135: *In baptismo Iohannis non erat peccati remissio.*
[193] C. 136: *Non solum originalis, sed etiam actualia peccata remittuntur in baptismate.*

baptism.[194] The rationale is that the charity of the church either relinquishes or holds sins.[195] Another way of stating this is that only Christ relinquishes sins.[196] As a consequence, the baptized in Christ are incorporated and made the members of Christ's body.[197]

Thirdly, baptism results in the working of grace in one's life which continues to relinquish sin. Baptism fulfills the law,[198] and the old infirmity, although not completely destroyed, loses its powers.[199] Being baptized is like becoming disciples of Christ, since Gratian states that the disciples of Christ are believed to be washed in baptism[200] and that all the apostles of Christ are believed to be baptized in baptism.[201] A heretic can perform the baptism on the Catholic catechumens,[202] and this does not

---

[194] C. 137: *Quicumque ex concupiscentia nascitur per baptismum regeneratur.* Cf. c. 2.
[195] C. 140: *Karitas ecclesiae peccata dimittit, vel tenet.*
[196] C. 141: *Solus Christus peccata dimittit.*
[197] Cc. 143-144: *Baptizati in Christo incorporantur, et eius membra fiunt.*
[198] C. 145: *Gratia non solum peccata dimittit, sed etiam legem inplere facit.*
[199] C. 146: *Vetus infirmitas in baptismo non penitus absumitur, sed vires amittit.*
[200] C. 147: *Discipuli Christi eius baptismate creduntur abluti.*
[201] C. 148: *Apostoli omnes Christi baptismate baptizati creduntur.*
[202] C. 149: *Catecuminus catholicus heretico baptizato*

diminish grace, since it is not the physical act and administration of the washing of body but the faith of the heart of the baptized that constitutes baptism.[203] Grace teaches what is sin, and, so that sin is avoided, grace works.[204] Without grace divine mandate cannot be fulfilled.[205]

In the course of his discussion, Gratian weaves the element of Christ's name and Trinity with the validity of baptism regardless of the human agents. Jesus Christ is the real minister of the valid baptism, whereas Trinity is the necessary substance of belief. Personal faith is crucial, although in some instances, faith of others suffices. Gratian presents his core concerns and resolves conflicts (regarding human performance of baptism and immersions, for example) by presenting what he considers the general rules and qualifying them with exceptions that account for conflicting sources.

Rather than presenting rules and exceptions that justify conflicting practices, Lombard considers all factors that validate a baptism. It is this preoccupation with validity or invalidity of the sacrament that per-

---

*prefertur.*
[203] C. 150: *Non tam ablutione corporis, quam fide cordis baptisma constitit.*
[204] C. 155: *Quid sit peccatum gratia docet, et ut vitetur facit.*
[205] C. 156: *Sine gratia divina mandata inpleri non possunt.*

vades his discussion more than the substantive content of Trinity and its doctrinal significance in baptism. In the course of his analysis, Lombard offers a logical format. In d. 2, he begins by distinguishing the sacrament of baptism from other rites, such as the Old Testament rite of circumcision and the baptism of John. In d. 3, he focuses on the positive aspects of baptism: what it is, what its form is, how it is performed (in the name of Christ), the institution of baptism, the use of water and immersion, relationship to circumcision, and the cause of the institution.

In d. 4, Lombard offers the distinction between the sacrament and *rem*. The sacrament refers to the act of baptism, whereas the *res* is the intended effect, the remission of sin. Lombard applies this distinction to explain questionable issues related to baptism, such as the effect of baptism undertaken fictitiously[206] and salvation absent baptism in exceptional cases (such as suffering for Christ and the case of infants).[207] Although this distinction between the *rem* and the sacrament does not originate with Lombard, he utilizes this technique to explain some fine distinctions, and utilizes the format of *determinatio* and *responsio* to deal with conflicting sources.

In d. 5, Lombard discusses the pro-

---

[206] D. 4. c. 2.
[207] D. 4. c. 4.

blem of agency: baptism administered by good versus evil men. This leads to the discussion of the power of baptism and its ministry. Lombard extends this discussion in d. 6, in cases where heretics administer baptism and whether rebaptism is necessary, such as in those cases where one is baptized in mother's womb or immersed in jest.

Lombard's discussion also demonstrates Lombard's familiarity with Gratian's text. He utilized some canons in similar contexts as Gratian and even integrated Gratian's dictum as part of his own opinion. For example, in c. 20, Gratian wrote that a woman should not presume to baptize.[208] In his dictum following the canon, Gratian wrote, "unless necessity forces otherwise."[209] In Lombard's discussion of who can baptize, he also includes this same canon followed by his comment that derives from Gratian's dictum.[210]

Despite this familiarity, the fact that Lombard differed from Gratian in approach and emphasis is revealing. In contrast to Gratian's approach, Lombard's discussion is in an evidently structured form. More substantively, comparison of Gratian's and Lombard's discussions on two classic issues

---

[208] *Non presumat mulier baptizare.*

[209] *Nisi necessitate cogente.*

[210] In d. 6. c. 1 at then end, Lombard cites from the Fifth Carthaginian Council ("Mulier, quamvis sancta, baptizare non praesumat") followed by his dictum, *"nisi necessitate cogente."*

related to baptism that contain contradictory positions show further implications of the differences of their approach. Regarding the Trinitarian formula and the element of faith, each offers unique insight by his method of approach. Explicitly, Gratian states in c. 1 that baptism and faith are necessary for salvation. Yet, he qualifies both, while the Trinity as the essence of baptism is apparent throughout Gratian's analysis. Gratian proceeds with this importance in his discussion of the mysteries signified at baptism and immersion. For Gratian, the invocation of the Trinitarian formula does not clash with the adequacy of the baptism in Christ's name, since they play different functions for a valid baptism. Furthermore, the persons of the Trinity are so closely bound together in a peculiar theological relationship that it is not contradictory to allow for both baptism in the name of Christ and baptism with the belief in the Trinity.

On the other hand, Lombard's key contribution is in the area of faith. While Gratian focuses on the object of faith (Trinity) more than the act of faith, to which Gratian pays cursory attention, Lombard focuses on the act of believing as essential. Consequently, Lombard gives a more detailed analysis on faith and the allowance for absence of it in the case of infants. Lombard's rem-sacramentum distinction is especially insightful in decoding the complexities related to the issue of faith and explaining the cases when it is not required.

Lombard, however, does not downplay the central role of the invocation of the Trinity as the determining factor for a valid baptism. Absence of the acknowledgment of the Trinity requires a rebaptism. That is the reason why John the Baptist's baptism was deficient as the sacrament of baptism in the remission of sin. While it pronounced and prepared for the baptism of Christ,[211] there was no cleansing of sin, since it was in water, not in the Spirit.[212] It was a baptism in penance, not in the remission of sins, like the baptism of Christ.[213] Because those baptized by John did not know or believe in the Holy Spirit, rebaptism was necessary because John's baptism was not the sacrament effective and adequate for salvation. Lombard also emphasizes the need to recognize the Trinity by stating that belief in Christ is not enough; those who do not believe in the Holy Spirit do not yet have clear eyes. Lombard gives an example of the Ephesians who were re-baptized because they did not hear of the Holy Spirit, even though they had received John's baptism.[214]

---

[211] D. 2. c. 2, c. 4.
[212] D. 2. c. 2.
[213] D. 2. c. 3.
[214] D. 2. c. 6.2: Unde Hieronymus, *Super Ioel*: << Qui dicit se in Christum credere, et non credit in Spiritum Sanctum, nondum habet claros oculos. Unde baptizati a Ioanne in nomine Venturi, id est

On the other hand, those who did not place hope in the baptism of John but believed the Father, Son and the Holy Spirit, were not afterwards baptized; but they received the Holy Spirit by the Apostle's imposition of hand.[215]

Furthermore, Lombard, also like Gratian, points out that baptism in Christ's name is just the same as baptism with the use of Trinitarian formula. In d. 3. c. 3, Lombard explains that the Apostles baptized in the name of Christ. But in this name, as Ambrose explains, is understood the whole Trinity: "For it is understood, when you say Christ, he is anointed with both the Father and the Holy Spirit."[216] Lombard also quotes from Pope Nicholas which concludes that whether they are baptized in the name of the holy Trinity or in the name of Christ, just as we read in the Acts of the Apostles, they are baptized. It is one and the same, as the holy Ambrose explains.[217]

---

Domini Iesu, quia dixerunt: *Sed neque si Spiritus Sanctus est audivimus*, iterum baptizantur, immo verum baptisma accipiunt>>.

[215] D. 2. c. 6.3: Illi vero qui spem non posuerunt in baptismo Ioannis, et Patrem et Filium et Spiritum Sanctum credebant, non post baptizati fuerunt; sed impositione manuum ab Apostolis super eos facta, Spiritum Sanctum receperunt. . . .

[216] Intelligitur enim, cum Christum dicis, et Pater a quo unctus est, et ipse qui unctus est, et Spiritus Sanctus per quem unctus est.

[217] D. 3. c. 3: Hi profecto, si in nomine sanctae Trinitatis, vel in nomine Christi, sicut in Actibus

This passage of Lombard seems to suggest that the invocation of "Christ" is sufficient, without the other persons, since in fact they are all one and the same, the basic import of the doctrine of Trinity.

However, although Lombard, like Gratian, emphasizes the component of the Trinity, he differs from Gratian. Lombard both points out a linguistic point in allowing for the interchangeability of using Christ's name or the invocation of Trinity and emphasizes the significance of faith for a valid baptism.

In d. 3, c. 4, Lombard starts by asking whether a baptism is valid if said in the name of the Father just as much as if said in the name of the Holy Spirit or of Christ.[218] He includes a passage from Ambrose to point out the theology of Trinity, three in one. He concludes that he who baptizes in the name of Christ does so in the name of Trinity, which is there understood. Lombard makes a linguistic note, that the baptism in the "name" (singular) is different than if the baptism is in "names" (plural). In the latter case, there is no sacrament since the correct form is not used.[219]

---

Apostolorum legimus, baptizentur, baptizati sunt. Unum enim diemque est, ut sanctus exponit Ambrosius.

[218] D. 3. c. 4.1: Hic quaeritur an baptismus esset verus, si diceretur in nomine Patris tantum vel Spiritus Sancti, ut cum dicitur in nomine Christi.

[219] D. 3. c. 4.5: Qui ergo baptizat in nomine Christi,

The important component apparent in his analysis of the Trinity is faith, which characterizes this sacrament. Lombard's focus on the element of faith with respect to the Trinity is apparent in another section of his discussion. Lombard quotes from Ambrose, which illustrates the element of faith:

Indeed, they denied that they knew the Holy Spirit, when they said that they were baptized by the baptism of John, which was in the advent of Jesus, not baptized in his name. They, since not in the name of Christ nor with the faith in the Holy Spirit they were baptized, they could not have received the sacrament of baptism. The baptized were therefore in the name of Christ. Nor is baptism to be repeated in these, but made new.[220]

---

baptizat in nomine Trinitatis, quando ibi intelligitur. Tutius est tamen tres personas ibi nominare, ut dicatur: *in nomine Patris et Filii et Spiritus Sancti*. -- Ambrosius in libro I De Spiritu Sancto: << Non in nominibus, sed *in nomine*>>, id est in invocatione vel in confessione Patris et Filii et Spiritus Sancti. Invocatur enim ibi Trinitas ut invisibiliter ibi operetur per se, sicut extra visibiliter per ministrum. Si autem dicatur *in nominibus*, non est ibi sacramentum, quia non servatur forma.

[220] D. 2. c. 6, c. 3: . . . . De hoc etiam Ambrosius: <<Quidam negaverunt se scire Spiritum Sanctum, cum baptizatos se dicerent Ioannis baptismo, qui in advenientis Iesu, non in suo baptizavit nomine. Isti ergo, quia nec in Christi nomine, nec cum fide Spiritus Sancti baptizati fuerant, non potuerunt accipere baptismi sacramentum. Baptizati sunt igitur in nomine Christi. Nec iteratum est in his baptisma,

In this passage, Lombard is not clear on whether the invocation of the three persons of the Trinity is necessary (d. 2. c. 6.2) for a valid baptism, or the invocation of the name of Christ, only one person, is sufficient. However, one thing is sure: receipt and knowledge of the Holy Spirit is a necessary element, without which baptism is not sufficient and a rebaptism is required. Lombard's focus is on the element of faith in the Holy Spirit. The absence of this important element was the reason for the inadequacy of John's baptism, since as John 1:31, 33 indicated, John's baptism differed from Christ's by the virtue of the fact that it was in water, not in Holy Spirit. The focus of Lombard's point seems to have been in the active faith in the Holy Spirit, a member of the Trinity. Once belief in Christ was premised on the knowledge of the nature of the Trinity, where Holy Spirit comprises one of three persons, then mere invocation of Christ, without the explicit reference to the others, is sufficient, because the tacit understanding is there.

Gratian, like Lombard, also points out the interchangeability of the baptism in Christ's name and baptism with the invocation of the Trinity. In c. 24, regarding the assertion stated by Gratian at the beginning of c. 23 that baptism is not repeated that

---

sed novatum.>>

which is administered by a pagan,[221] Gratian mentions from the canons a statement which indicates the equality of invocation of either the name of the Trinity or the name of Christ by which there is baptism, since they are one and the same, and there ought to be no rebaptism.[222] Furthermore in c. 30, although Gratian titles this as stating that they are proved to be baptized who are baptized in the name of the Lord,[223] Gratian cites from the canons a passage that suggests that there must be rebaptism if the baptism in question is not in the name of the Trinity.[224] In cc. 28-29, Gratian more explicitly asserts that baptisms are not repeated which are performed in the name of the Trinity.[225] In still another canon, Gratian claims that even baptism by heretics but in the name of

---

[221] C. 23: *Non reiteretur baptisma, quod a pagano ministratur.*

[222] C. 24: . . . . Hi profecto, si in nomine S. Trinitatis, uel tantum in Christi nomine, sicut in Actibus Apostolorum legitur, baptizati sunt (unum quippe idemque est, ut sanctus Ambrosius exponit) quia non illorum, sed eius est, rebaptizari non debent.

[223] C. 30: *Baptizantur qui tantum in nomine Domini baptizati probantur.*

[224] C. 30: . . . . Si revera hi de hereticis, qui in locis dilectioni tuae vicinis conmorari dicuntur, solummodo se in nomine Domini baptizatos fuisse forsitan confitentur, sine cuiusquam dubitationis ambiguo eos ad catholicam fidem venientes S. Trinitatis nomine baptizabis. . . .

[225] C. 28: *Non reiteratur baptisma, quod in nomine S. Trinitatis prestatur.*

Trinity is received in the church.[226] By these series of statements, Gratian confirms that baptism performed in the name of Christ is not different in nature from baptism with the invocation of the Trinity. Gratian's juxtapositioning of these two statements seem to suggest that Christ, as part of the Trinity, can stand for the Trinity, the whole and which is an absolutely necessary theological component of baptism.

Although both Gratian and Lombard use similar canons to come to a similar conclusion about the Trinity, their different methods illustrate varying emphases. For example, the canon Gratian cites in c. 24 is also cited by Lombard in d. 3. c. 3. Gratian places the canon in the context of his discussion of agency. From c. 19, Gratian provides exceptions to the rule that only priests should presume to baptize. The critical test is not the identity of the agents administering the sacrament, but the virtue of Christ operating in baptism, since Christ is the true administrator of the valid sacrament.[227]

In this context regarding the irrelevance of agents, Gratian includes c. 24 from the canons. The passage that Gratian quotes differs, slightly but significantly,

---

[226] C. 44: *Quomodo recipiantur in ecclesia qui in nomine Trinitatis apud hereticos baptizantur*.

[227] C. 39: *Et per bonos et per malos ministros eque baptizat Christus* (underscoring mine).

from that which Lombard uses. Under the heading that "baptism is not repeated, that which is administered by a pagan," [228] Gratian in c. 24 quotes this passage with slight modifications. A juxtaposition of the two passages show the differences in the passages as cited by Gratian and Lombard:

> *Gratian:*
> A quodam Iudeo, <u>nescitis utrum Christiano, an pagano</u>, multos in patria vestra baptizatos asseritis, et quid inde sit agendum consulitis. Hi profecto, si in nomine S. Trinitatis, vel tantum in Christi nomine, sicut in Actibus Apostolorum legitur, baptizati sunt (unum quippe idemque est, ut sanctus Ambrosius exponit) quia non illorum, sed eius est, rebaptizari non debent.[229]
>
> *Lombard:*
> A quodam Iudaeo multos baptizatos asseritis, et quid inde agendum sit consulitis.

---

[228] C. 23: *Non reiteretur baptisma, quod a pagano minstratur*. [Note that the heading of c. 24 is *De eodem*, referring to the previous title].
[229] *Decreto* Gratiani, *de consecr.* d. 4, c. 24 (1368), underscoring mine.

> Hi profecto, si in nomine sanctate Trinitatis, vel in nomine Christi, sicut in Actibus Apostolorum legimus, baptizentur, baptizati sunt. Unum enim idemque est, ut sanctus exponit Ambrosis.[230]

Lombard also quotes the original source, Ambrose.[231] However, Gratian includes the phrase *"nescitis utrum Christiana, an pagano"* and emphasizes that there ought to be no baptism. For Gratian, the issue of being baptized in the name of Trinity as equaling that in the name of Christ takes on the further significance of being so crucial and definitive that even if the agent was unknown, no re-baptism is necessary. While Lombard uses a truncated version of this passage to make one point, Gratian links it with the issue of agency.

This clarity and forcefulness with respect to the element of Trinity in baptism is further reinforced in Gratian's positioning of the canon regarding the use of vulgar Latin in the invocation of the Trinity. Both Gratian[232] and Lombard[233] include a passage from the canons in the case of an ignorant

---

[230] Peter Lombard, *Sent.* 4. d. 3, c. 3, 2:245.
[231] D. 3. c. 3.
[232] c. 86.
[233] d. 6. c. 4.1.

priest who invokes the Trinity as "Patria, Filia, Spiritus sancta." When a priest does so out of ignorance, there should be no rebaptism because the baptism is valid. However, if the priest does so to introduce error or heresy, then rebaptism is necessary because there is intent to mislead on the part of the priest.

Again, both include the passage and come to the same conclusion. However, the contexts of these passages reveal differences in their approach. Whereas Gratian's concern is with the substance of the Trinity, Lombard's concern is with the form of words and the his resolution of the problem regarding infants and the exemption of faith. Gratian introduces the case of erroneous words due to ignorance (in c. 73), and before he comments again on the effect of vulgar use of Latin in the invocation of the Trinity in c. 86, Gratian considers the mysteries signified at the font of baptism and the problem of immersion, which illustrates the doctrinal content of the Trinity.

In reply to the inquiry posed in c. 73 regarding the mysteries present at baptism, Gratian provides a canon that includes interrogations of the ones to be baptized. Here, Gratian shows how the presence of the Trinity consecrates the font of baptism. After posing the statement, what mysteries signify that which are celebrated in the font of baptism, [234] Gratian quotes from St. Augustine which includes the belief regarding the Trinity:

> We asked, do you believe in the God the Father omnipotent? You responded, I believe. Again we asked, do you believe in Jesus Christ his son, who was born of the Holy Spirit and of Virgin Mary? You responded, I believe. Again we asked, and in Holy Spirit? You responded similarly, I believe.[235]

Lombard also uses a sentence from this source, but in another context. He quotes only one sentence, which in Gratian's text precedes the questions asked at interrogation regarding the respondent's beliefs. Lombard chooses only the following sentence: "You uttered the most certain provision, by which you vowed to renounce the vanities of the

---

[234] c. 73: *Quid significent misteria, que in fonte baptismatis celebrantur.*

[235] c. 73: . . . . interrogavimus: Credis in Deum Patrem omnipotentem? Respondistis: Credo. Rursum interrogavimus: Credis et in Iesus Christum filium eius, qui natus est de Spiritu sancto et Maria Virgine? Respondistis singuli: Credo. Item interrogavimus: et in Spiritum sanctum? Respondistis similiter: Credo. . . .

devil."[236]

While Gratian quotes a lengthy section from Augustine to indicate that belief in the three persons of the Trinity, the fundamental mysteries present at baptism, is necessary, Lombard, although acknowledging the centrality of Trinity elsewhere, does not include the subsequent response of faith in the Trinity, but chooses this sentence which shows the *effect* of a certain form of words. In fact, the context of this passage in Lombard is a discussion of the sense of words[237] and what is meant by *fidem, credo, fidem peto,* and *credo in Deum Patrem et in Iesus Christum et in Spiritum sanctum.*

Furthermore, Lombard here focuses on the subject of his emphasis, the problem of infants and faith. He explains that those coming to be baptized ought to profess their faith and explain what they came to seek at the church. If the person is an adult, he should respond on his own, that he came to seek faith, that is the sacrament of faith and doctrine. He alone ought to be interrogated and he should respond that he believes in the Father and the Son, and so forth. If the person is an infant, who is not in the capacity to believe or to speak, another should respond on his behalf.[238] On the other hand, Gratian

---

[236] D. 6. c. 6.3: Certissimam emistis cautionem, qua renuntiare pompis diaboli spopondistis.

[237] D. 6. c. 6: *de sensu verborum.*

[238] d. 6. c. 6. 1: De responsione patrinorum. Porro

is more interested in the content and substance of Trinity than the form of words. Whether the Trinity formula is professed by the baptized or by someone else in exceptional cases, it has to exist at baptism in some for or other.

This focus on the substance of the Trinity is apparent in Gratian's discussion of immersion that is surrounded by his two statements regarding the irrelevance of the erroneous words as a result of ignorance. Regarding how many times one can be immersed in baptism (cc. 78-85), Gratian and Lombard both agree in providing for three-time or one time immersion. However, the emphases are different. Gratian starts out with the premise that three-times is, as a rule, practiced. In c. 78, the beginning of his discussion on immersion (cc. 78-85), he asks why three time immersion is celebrated in baptism.[239] He states at the end of his discussion that it is permitted to immerse once in baptism.[240]

---

cuncti ad baptismum venientes fidem suam profiteri debent, et exponere quid petere venerint ad ecclesiam. Unde et a baptizando quaeritur: Quid venisti ad ecclesiam petere? Qui, si adultus est, pro se respondet: Fidem, id est sacramentum fidei et doctrinam. Ita etiam per singula interrogatus, respondet se credere in Patrem et Filium etc. Si autem parvulus est, non valens credere vel loqui, alius pro eo respondet.
[239] *Quare trina mersio in baptismate celebretur.*
[240] *Semel in baptismate mergere licet.*

In contrast, Lombard, at the beginning of his discussion on immersion in d. 3. c. 7 begins with the following:

> Regarding immersion, if it is asked how many times precisely it ought to be made, we respond: either once or three times according to the various customs of the churches.[241]

It is at the end of his discussion that Lombard uses the Augustine's source that Gratian includes first in c. 78.

Gratian's selection of Augustine's text in c. 78 includes further explanation for the significance of the three immersion. The significance of the three-day burial of Christ is heightened by the fact that the baptized are considered buried with Christ in baptism, resurrected with Christ in faith, absolved of sins, and imitating the sanctity of the virtue of Christ.[242] Gratian includes this passage about the theological significance of thrice immersion and what it signifies to actual life, while Lombard does not, since his focus is

---

[241] D. 3. c. 7.1: De immersione vero, si quaeritur quomodo fieri debeat praecise, respondemus: vel semel, vel tertio, pro vario more Ecclesiae.
[242] C. 78: . . . . per quam Christo consepulti estis in baptismo, et cum Christo resurrexistis in fide, ut peccatis absoluti in sanctitate virtutum Christum vivatis imitando.

on the validity of baptism, and either once or thrice immersion fulfills the requirement.

Lombard places emphasis on the equally valid methods of immersion (once or three times) by his selectivity and positioning of another cited authority. Both Gratian[243] and Lombard[244] cite from Gregory. The passage supports diverse practice in different churches. However, Lombard rearranges a section of the passage so that the last part in Gratian's cite is quoted earlier in his selection:

> For since in three subsistence is one substance, it is reprehensible that one could not immerse either thrice or once in baptism: since in three immersions the Trinity of persons could be designated, and in one, the singularity of divinity.[245]

Lombard inserts this and omits a sentence in Gratian's citation,[246] indicating the prefer-

---

[243] In c. 80.
[244] In d. 3. c. 7.1.
[245] d. 3. c. 7.1: . . . . Quia enim in tribus subsistentiis una substantia est, reprehensibile esse nullatenus potest infantem in baptismo vel ter vel semel mergere: quia et in tribus mersionibus personarum trinitas, et in una potest divinitatis singularitas designari. . . .
[246] C. 80: "Nos autem, quod tertio mergimus,

ence of the writer to the thrice rule.

Besides the signification of the three-day burial of Christ and believers in Christ in the three time immersion, Gratian also provides a further theological point favoring the three-time immersion. In c. 85, Gratian includes a letter of Pope Zecharias to Boniface in order to prove his assertion that in the invocation of the Trinity we ought to immerse three times in baptism.[247] Lombard also includes a portion of this passage earlier in his discussion on the forms of baptism, which specify the need to invoke the three persons of the Trinity.[248] However, Gratian's use of this passage specifically on immersion favors the three-time practice because of its signification of the necessary Trinity formula in the act of immersion. Gratian continues in c. 84 to point out that those who are not baptized in the name of the Trinity are to be rebaptized.[249]

Furthermore, in c. 81, when Gratian continues his presentation of canons regarding those who are merged once in baptism (cc. 79-80), Gratian cites Jerome indicating the practice of immersion three times which signify three person of the Trinity. Jerome stated that this is permitted on account of the

---

triduanae sepulturae sacramenta signamus".
[247] *In invocatione Trinitatis tertio in baptismate mergere debemus.*
[248] D. 3. c. 2.
[249] *Rebaptizentur, qui in nomine Trinitatis baptizati non fuerint.*

Trinity; nevertheless, it is reputed to be one baptism, and not three. Although the Latin word used is *"baptizetur"* instead of *"mergetur,"* three time *immersion* is implied, since the heading under which Gratian cites the canon addresses particular issues of thrice immersion.[250] Gratian's juxtaposition of this passage in this context is interesting. He combines the concept of three immersion and one baptism in one, and thus makes a strong theological point about Trinity (three persons in one). Just as three immersions comprise one baptism, and not three, so the three persons of the Trinity comprise one deity.

On the other hand, Lombard discusses this passage about thrice immersion representing one baptism in the context of cases regarding the issue of when rebaptism is necessary. As an addendum, Lombard seems to distinguish immersions versus baptism, whereas Gratian employs this passage to insinuate the significance of the Trinity. Lombard states that certain words are required for a valid baptism,[251] but the case of vulgar use of Latin is a distinguishing case. After presenting the issue of heretics' administering baptism, infants baptized in

---

[250] Cc. 79-81: *De his, qui semel, non tertio in baptismate merguntur* (underscoring mine).

[251] D. 3. c. 1.2: . . . . Baptismus dicitur tinctio, id est ablutio corporis exterior, facta sub forma verborum praescripta. . . .

the wombs of their mothers and baptisms done in jest, Lombard discusses this issue of vulgar use of Latin in the invocation of the Trinity. The text which Gratian uses supports the Trinitarian theology present in baptism, while Lombard uses it in another place dealing with the validity of the sacrament and cases where rebaptism is necessary.

In c. 82, Gratian further augments the position of three immersion by quoting Pelagius. Although many practice a one-time immersion, the evangelical precept indicates three times in the name of the Trinity, as Jesus himself said to his disciples to baptize all nations in the name of the Father, the Son and the Holy Spirit. As the passage that Gratian selects and includes indicates, three times is closely bound with the theological point of the Trinity. This is the rule, not just one of two equal options.

This perspective is even further supported in the next canon that Gratian includes. In c. 83, Gratian states that in the invocation of the Trinity, we ought to immerse three times in baptism.[252] He uses this heading to cite a passage that puts forth a strong argument for the invocation of the Trinity as necessary. The canon sets forth a strong case that the invocation of Trinity is absolutely necessary for the baptism to be a

---

[252] C. 83: *In invocatione Trinitatis tertio in baptismate mergere debemus.*

sacrament of regeneration. Without this, there is no perfected Christian. He who names only one person of the Trinity in baptism has not undertaken a true baptism. Since he who confesses the Father and the Son but not the Holy Spirit neither has the Father nor the Son, and he who confessed the Father and the Holy Spirit but not the Son has neither the Father nor the Holy Spirit, and the divine grace is void.[253] The canon deals with the theology of Trinity, not immersion. But by utilizing an authority about the Trinity to support his point on the thrice immersion,[254] Gratian proposes the standard of thrice immersion. In effect, he suggests that three-time immersion is normally virtually tantamount to confession of the three persons of the Trinity.

This point is further elaborated in the next canon, c. 84, where Gratian states that, they are rebaptized who were not baptized in the name of the Trinity.[255] In the midst of presenting canons on the immersion in a

---

[253] C. 83: . . . . Quod pro certo verum est, quia, qui unum ex sancta Trinitate confessus non fuerit nomen, perfectus Christianus esse non potest. Qui enim confitetur Patrem et Filium, si confessus non fuerit Spiritum sanctum, neque Patrem habet, neque Filium; et qui confessus fuerit Patrem et Spiritum sanctum, et Filium non fuerit confessus, neque Patrem habet, neque Spiritum sanctum, sed vacuus est divina gratia.
[254] C. 83: *In invocatione* <u>Trinitatis</u> *tertio in baptismate mergere debemus* (underscoring mine).
[255] C. 84: *Rebaptizentur qui in nomine Trinitatis baptizati non fuerint.*

baptism and the close connection between three times and the confession of the three persons of the Trinity, Gratian provides a canon that indicates that baptism without the invocation of the Trinity is invalid as a sacrament. By inference, in the line of his arguments, given that the three time immersion signifies the belief in the Trinity, anything other than the three time immersion that discredits the proper view of the Trinity is invalid as a sacrament. Gratian is not inferring that failure to immerse three times automatically signifies a lack of confession in the Trinity; but he is hinting that it is more likely that in an one-time immersion, one could easily overlook the significance of the Trinity.

In the last canon regarding the immersion issue in this section, Gratian does provide for what amounts to as an exception, that it is permitted to immerse once in baptism in certain cases. [256] The canon provides that it is on account of avoiding the scandal of schismatics or the use of heretical dogmas that a simple immersion of baptism is held.[257] There is no further elaboration or inclusion on this point, and earlier consideration of one-time immersion emphasized the three time immersion, although

---

[256] C. 85: *Semel in baptismate mergere licet.*
[257] C. 85: Propter vitandum scismatis scandalum, vel heretici dogmatis usum, simplam teneamus baptismi mersionem.

diverse churches did otherwise, not as a denial of the Trinity but as its own local custom, for whatever reason. At any rate Gratian's view of the closeness of the connection between the number of immersion and confession of Trinity is so close that he opts for the safer road of three-times immersion as the rule.

Although Lombard's treatment of the theology of Trinity in baptism is more in terms of the form of words than in the substance of the doctrine, Lombard's discussion of the tension between faith and the case of infants is profound. In contrast, Gratian does not pay much attention to the phenomenon of faith, as opposed to the object of faith. He simply states that faith is necessary, along with baptism, for salvation (c. 1), and poses the situation of infants as an exception to that general rule. In the case of infants, the faith of those presenting the infants is sufficient (c. 7), and that baptism is considered adequate toward salvation, even if faith requirement is missing (c. 33). He reiterates this concept in c. 74, where he states that infants are baptized by the faith of others. Near the end of his discussion in cc. 138-139, Gratian again states that the faith of the ones bringing the infants to baptism is enough. The weak, mute and deaf can also be baptized by the faith of others, and Gratian emphasizes that it is the sacrament of faith, not the faith itself, that makes the infant faithful (c. 76).

Gratian also implicitly states that another case of an exception to this general rule. In c. 34, he asserts that the shedding of blood is an adequate substitute for baptism. He includes a canon that Lombard later uses in greater depth. This authority represents the complex issue of the necessity of faith and baptism and the fact that in some cases where either one or both are missing there is still salvation. However, Gratian does not give much commentary on this complex issue of the exceptions to the rule requiring faith and baptism.

On the other hand, Lombard's focus on faith gives insight into the complex theological implications of the requirement of faith. He resolves conflicts regarding this issue by focusing on the *rem* (grace of remission) and the sacrament itself. Adults who are baptized receive both if they have faith,[258] although infants may have both with the faith of another.[259] In general, however, those who approach without faith or fictitiously, receive the sacrament but not the *rem*.[260] This faith generally involves

---

[258] D. 4. c. 1.2: Adulti quoque qui cum fide baptizantur, sacramentum et rem suscipiunt.
[259] D. 4. c. 2. 3: . . . . quia nec parvulis sine fide aliena, qui propriam habere nequeunt, datur in baptismo remissio.
[260] D. 4. c. 2.1: Qui vero sine fide accedunt vel ficte, sacramentum, non rem suscipiunt.

penance,[261] which also means having true contrition of heart.[262]

There are others who, on the other hand, receive the *rem* and not the sacrament. For instance, suffering for Christ fulfills the function of baptism.[263] Lombard includes a passage from Augustine's *City of God*, which states that when one dies in confession of Christ, their sins are relinquished, as if they are washed at the sacred font of baptism. This passion *pro nomine Iesu* fulfills the function of baptism. Also, faith and contrition standing alone fulfills the function of baptism, where necessity excludes the sacrament.[264] Augustine gave the example of the thief on the cross. Here is the case, where although *sine visibili baptismi sacramento*, there is remission of

---

[261] D. 4. c. 2.2: . . . . nisi poeniteat eum veteris vitae, novam non potest inchoare. Ab hac poenitentia, cum baptizantur, soli parvuli immunes sunt.

[262] Lombard summarizes the prior statements in the following, d. 4. c. 2.3: Hi aliisque testimoniis aperte ostenditur adultis sine fide et poenitudine vera in baptismo non conferri gratiam remissionis, quia nec parvulis sine fide aliena, qui propriam habere nequeunt, datur in baptismo remissio. Si quis ergo ficte accedat, non habens cordis veram contritionem, sacramentum sine re accipit.

[263] D. 4. c. 4.1: Qui enim effundunt sanguinem pro nomine Iesus, etsi non sacramentum, rem tamen percipiunt.

[264] D. 4. c. 4.3: Nec tantum passio vicem baptismi implet, sed etiam fides et contritio, ubi necessitas excludit sacramentum, sicut aperte docet Augustinus. . . .

sin. Although Gratian includes this passage in c. 34, Lombard's *rem-sacramentum* distinction as applied here is insightful in the resolution and justification of the disparity between the rule that visible sacrament is necessary for salvation and its exceptions.

Lombard takes this passage further by including Augustine's modification of the example of thief in his *Retractions*:

> In the fourth book regarding baptism, when I said that suffering could have the function of baptism, I did not place the example of the thief suitably enough, since it is not certain whether he was not baptized.[265]

This reinforces the argument that one can receive the *rem* (remission of sin) without the sacrament of baptism. For if that were not possible, Augustine would not have felt the need to retract just in case the thief might have had been baptized. Lombard further quotes Ambrose to illustrate justification and salvation without baptism.[266]

---

[265] D. 4. c. 4.4: <<In quarto libro *De baptismo*, cum dicerem vicem baptismi posse habere passionem, non satis posui idoneum illius latornis exemplum, quia utrum non fuerit baptizatus incertum est.>>

[266] D. 4. c. 4. 5: Constat igitur sine baptismo aliquos iustificari et salvari. Unde Ambrosius de Valentiniano: << *Ventrem meum doleo*, ut prophetico

He presents the problem, in d. 4. c. 4.6, created by the conflicting text in the Bible where Jesus Himself said that "unless one is not born of the water and the Holy Spirit, he cannot enter the kingdom of heaven" (John 3:5)[267] and continues his discussion to reconcile the conflicts. He determines that the regeneration in question is not made only through baptism, but also through penance and blood.[268] He argues this point on the fact that *ratio etiam id suadet*. If baptism is sufficient for infants who are not capable of believing, how much more is the faith sufficient for the willing adults, but not in the position to be baptized.[269] By quoting Augustine and his use of Scripture (Jon 11:25 where Christ said, One who believed in me will live even if dies),[270] Lombard

---

utar eloquio, quia quem regeneraturus eram amisi; ille tamen gratiam quam poposcit non amisit>>.

[267] D. 4. c. 4.6: His autem videtur obviare quod Dominus ait: *Nisi quis renatus fuerit ex aqua et Spiritu Sancto, non potest introire in regnum caelorum.* Quod si generaliter verum est, non videntur esse vera superius posita.

[268] D. 4. c. 4.7: . . . . Illa autem regeneratio fit non tantum per baptismum, sed etiam per poenitentiam et sanguinem.

[269] D. 4. c. 4.8: . . . . Si enim parvulis non valentibus credere sufficit baptismus, multo magis sufficit fides adultis volentibus, sed non valentibus baptizari.

[270] D. 4. c. 4.8: . . . . In libro De unico baptismo. Unde Augustinus: <<Quaeris quid sit maius, fides an aqua? Non dubito quin respondeam fidem. Si ergo quod minus est sanctificare potest, nonne quod maius est, id est fides, de qua Christus ait: *Qui crediderit in*

puts more emphasis on the faith aspect. Whereas Gratian holds firmly to the necessity of baptism, even if without faith for infants, Lombard emphasizes the importance of faith, even if there is no baptism.

Lombard presents other authorities that conflict with his statement. These sources state that suffering is the only exception to the necessity of baptism for salvation.[271] Lombard answers with an Augustinian quotation that if anyone having faith and charity wished to be baptized and could not because necessity prevented it, the kindness of the Almighty supplies what is lacking in the sacrament.[272] He further quotes from Augustine that although invisible sanctification is possible with the visible sacrament, visible sacrament without the invisible is not useful.[273] Faith is more important than the visible sacrament.

Then Lombard quotes from a passage of Augustine which Gratian also

---

*me, etiam si mortuus fuerit, vivet?>>*
[271] D. 4. c. 4.9: Sed dicunt aliqui nullum adultum in Christum credere vel caritatem habere sine baptismo, nisi sanguinem fundat pro Domino; subdit introducentes testimonia.
[272] D. 4. c. 4.10: . . . . Si enim aliquis habens fidem et caritatem voluerit baptizari, et non potest, necessitate praeventus, (Augustinus:) <<supplet Omnipotentis benignitas quod sacramento defuerat.>>
[273] D. 4. c. 4.11: <<Sine visibili ergo invisibilis sanctificatio esse potest et prodesse; visibilis autem, quae fit sacramentotenus, sine invisibili prodesse non potest, cum ista sit omnis illius utilitas. . . .>>

includes near the beginning of his discussion on baptism (c. 3). Lombard precedes this passage by saying that another's faith does not fare so much for the infant as much as one's own faith for the adult, since the faith of the Church is not sufficient without the sacrament, and those who died without baptism will be damned.[274] The following is his quotation:

> Firmissime tene parvulos qui vel in uteris matrum vivere incipiunt et ibi moriuntur, vel de matribus nati sine sacramento baptismi de hoc saeculo transeunt, aeterno supplicio puniendos: quia etsi peccatum propriae actionis non habuerunt, originale tamen peccatum carnali conceptione traxerunt.[275]
>
> [*Hold most firmly that infants who begin to live in the wombs of their mothers and die there or are born from mother cross over to this*

---

[274] D. 4. c. 4.12: Nec tantum valet fides aliena parvulo, quantum propria adulto. Parvulis enim non sufficit fides Ecclesiae sine sacramento. Qui si absque baptismo fuerint defuncti, etiam cum deferuntur ad baptismum, damnabuntur, sicut multis Sanctorum testimoniis comprobatur.
[275] D. 4. c. 4.12.

> *world without the sacrament of baptism will be punished with eternal punishment, since even if they did not have sins of their own actions, they nevertheless assumed original sin by carnal conception.*]

Lombard quotes this text in support of the absolute necessity and predominance of faith. The case of infants, for Lombard, illustrates the importance of faith, without which another's faith in the absence of baptism is not adequate.

On the other hand, Gratian presents this same text, with slight, significant, variations, to point out the importance of *baptism* for salvation, since one conceived from man and woman is born with original sin and *nec sine baptismate saluatur*.[276] He had started his discussion with the rule that *sine sacramento visibili et fide invisiblili nemo saluatur*[277] and then continued with the statement that concupiscence is extinguished in baptism.[278] In c. 3, where Gratian cites authority also present in Lombard's discussion, he includes words that Lombard omits. The underlined portions indicate these words missing in Lombard's

---

[276] C. 3.
[277] C. 1.
[278] C. 2.

selection:

> .... Firmissime tene, <u>non solum homines ratione utentes, uerum etiam</u> parvulos, qui sive in uteris matrum vivere incipiunt, et ibi moriuntur, sive iam de matribus nati sine baptismatis sacramento<u>, quod datur in nomine Patris, et Filii, et Spiritus sancti</u>, de hoc seculo transeunt, <u>sempiterno igne</u> puniendos; quia, etsi peccatum propriae actionis nullum habent, originalis tamen peccati <u>dampnationem</u> carnali conceptione ex nativitate traxerunt.[279]

In the above underlined phrases, the significant differences from Lombard are with respect to the first two. Lombard started his discussion regarding all men in general, whereas Gratian's version includes the text that indicates his focus on infants, *as well as* the adults. His emphasis is in the necessity of baptism, whether it be adults or infants, who are born in sin. Lombard, on the other hand, omits reference to all people in general, and focuses on infants, who are the focus of his concern. By doing that,

---

[279] C. 3, underscoring mine.

Lombard gives emphasis in the case of infants that proves that baptism is not absolutely necessary in all circumstances. Furthermore, Lombard uses this passage to support his contention that if baptism of infants without their own faith is adequate (as this passage suggests), faith of adults without baptism is even more sufficient.

Secondly, Gratian includes the Trinitarian formula, whereas Lombard does not. From the outset of his discussion, Gratian places emphasis on the essential component of the Trinity in the sacrament of baptism. In fact, immediately before Gratian begins his discussion of baptism, he states the belief in the faith of the Trinity and unity [of the Deity] at the end of *Distinctio* 3, in c. 30.[280] Although Lombard too does not neglect to consider the verbal formula of Trinity as indispensable element of baptism, Lombard's primary concern here, in d. 4. c. 4.12 [*Firmissime tene*, etc.], is with the faith that saves *absent* baptism, hence his omission of this formula as being irrelevant to his discussion.

Lombard ends his discussion in d. 4. c. 4 by concluding that just as infants who die without baptism are ascribed with the number of infidels, thus those baptized are called faithful. Since they are not separated from the consort of the faithful when the

---

[280] D. 3. c. 30: *De fide Trinitatis et Unitatis inviolabiliter servanda.*

Church prays on behalf of the faithful ones who are dead, the faithful ones have not become faithful on account of virtue, but on account of the sacrament of faith. Lombard quotes Augustine to point out the fact that the baptism is that of faith which makes one faithful.[281] The significance and effect of baptism is not so much in creating faith, but giving more to those who already have faith; it nourishes and gives helping grace and virtue.[282]

Gratian states a similar assertion regarding grace in the context of baptism at the end of his discussion. He writes that grace relinquishes sins and helps so that sins are not repeated.[283] Grace teaches what is sin, and so that sin is avoided, grace works.[284] Finally, without grace divine

---

[281] D. 4. c. 4.13: Et sicut parvuli qui sine baptismo moriuntur numero infidelium adscribuntur, ita qui baptizantur fideles vocantur. Quia a fidelium consortio non separantur cum orat Ecclesia pro fidelibus defunctis; fideles igitur sunt non propter virtutem, sed fidei sacramentum. -- Augustinus, ad Bonifacium. Unde Augustinus: <<Parvulum, etsi nondum fides illa quae in credentium voluntate consistit, iam tamen ipsius fidei sacramentum, id est baptismus, fidelem facit. Sicut credere respondetur, ita etiam fidelis vocatur: non rem ipsam mente annuendo, sed ipsius rei sacramentum percipiendo.>>
[282] D. 4. c. 5.
[283] C. 154: *Gratia et peccata dimittit, et ne reiterentur adiuvat.*
[284] C. 155: *Quid sit peccatum gratia docet, et ut vitetur facit.*

mandates could not be fulfilled.[285]

With respect to these fundamental issues of grace, importance of the invocation of the Trinity at baptism, and the significance of the element of faith, Gratian and Lombard do not differ in their final conclusions. Rather, what is intriguing in the comparison between the two's discussions on baptism are their varying methods of approach, their emphases, and their contributions.

Gratian is concerned with harmonizing many authorities, often conflicting. In the process, Gratian utilizes the tactic of setting forth the rule and providing exceptions to the rule. Gratian takes a more rigorous position on the theological significance of the need of baptism and the presence of Trinity at baptism. Hence, he centers his presentation around the premise that baptism is absolutely necessary for salvation, although he includes one canon that provides one substitution. He utilizes infant baptism to indicate the necessity of baptism, regardless of faith. He employs the agency principle to emphasize that baptism in Christ's name is valid regardless of human agents. He skillfully structures his analysis of baptism so that Trinitarian motifs are ever present. Agents are irrelevant, as long as the baptism in Christ contains the

---

[285] C. 156: *Sine gratia divina mandata inpleri non possunt.*

element of Trinity, whether in explicit invocation or tacit understanding. Words of the Trinity could even be erroneous, as long as the Trinity is meant. The rule of immersion is presented as being thrice, although one-time immersion is also practiced in some cases, since the number of immersions parallels the three persons of the Trinity. Furthermore, the questions asked at baptism first deal with the belief in the Trinity, whose presence graces the font of baptism.

On the other hand, Lombard is more sparing in the inclusion of sources, although he deals with the ones he uses closely. His concern is less with the harmony of all possible sources and conflicts, but with presenting the factors that validate a baptism and conditions that lead to salvation. Along these lines, Lombard considers either thrice or once immersion as equally valid; he shows no preference to either, since each is sufficient for a valid baptism. His requirements for a valid baptism concern the use of proper or permissible language and the act of washing. Furthermore, more than with the object and content of belief, he deals more with the act of faith and the limited value of baptism. Baptism brings salvation for the baptized only when faith is also present; however, baptism is not absolutely necessary for salvation. One can attain salvation without baptism, as with people who suffer for Christ or have faith and contrition where there is no opportunity for baptism. The fact that infants are baptized without personal professing faith proves for Lombard how much more possible is salvation without baptism, so long as the adults have professing faith. Hence, he does not associate salvation only with baptism, because there are other factors present that allow for salvation in the absence of baptism. Utilizing the *rem-sacramentum* analysis, Lombard finely distinguishes different situations of salvation despite absence of baptism and baptism without salvation.

Ironically, although Gratian is considered a major figure in canon law and Lombard is an influential "theologian," Gratian, in his discussion of the sacrament of baptism, primarily focuses on the theological issues of Trinity, while Lombard's analysis, probing the validity of the sacrament, is legal in nature. This indicates not only the fluidity between the theology and canon law disciplines even in the twelfth century, a period of the flowering of legal renaissance, but also the multi-faceted characteristics of medieval canon law.

# The Order of the Templars and their Criminalization in the 14th Century AD

The Parisian authorities, under the direction of King Philip the IV and the Grand Inquisitor of France, Guillaume de Nogaret, arrested some members of the Order of the Temple in October 13 (Friday) of 1307. In the first round of depositions in the following October and November of 1307, 134 out of 138 deposed Templars confessed to the charges of denying God, spitting on the crucifix, obscene kissing, homosexuality and/or idol worship. The Order dissolved in 1312 after further arrests and depositions, confessions before the University of Paris and the papal commission, defenses by a number of the Templars, the Council of Vienne in 1311, and the burning of prominent Templars, including the Grand Master, Jacobus de Molay.

The trial of the Templars, for many scholars, represents a classic case of a political witchcraft trial, whereby the authorities cast one group of people as witches, or dangerous outcasts, in order to discredit their legitimacy and justify the use of force to suppress their livelihood as members of the group. This paper, on the other hand, will argue that rather than *maleficia* (witchcraft) specifically, blasphemy is the persistently underlying theme throughout the whole process, from the depictions of a blasphemous group that led to both the arrests and to the final dissolution, to the charges of and confessions to the sins of the mouth (abnegations, spitting, kissing and lying) in the initial stage of the process which shaped the tenor of the whole trial.

The Order of the Temple, founded in 1119, was a military order created for the purpose of protecting Christian crusaders in the Holy Land. The Order received papal approval and protection, and like other religious orders, vowed to obedience, poverty and chastity. They further engaged in economic enterprises that were successful and played a vital role in the finance department of the French monarchy.

Their legitimacy and relevance was subject to severe doubt after 1291, when Acre fell to the Muslims under al-Asraf the sultan. Nevertheless, up to the day before the first round of arrests, the members, who were actively engaged in other affairs of business and finance, had no reason to suspect their fatal outcome at the hands of the French monarchy. The day before the arrests on October 13, 1307, the Grand

Master took part in the wedding feast in the French king's palace.

Behind the whole affair was the political interests of Philip the IV, the French king for whom the Order was a hindrance to his political ambitions. For instance, Philip wanted to create a super Order combining various military orders with Philip at the head, but the Order of the Temple refused to cooperate.[286] The very existence of the Order thwarted the political ambitions of the monarchy, and the Order had to be destroyed.

The French authorities needed to demonstrate the legitimacy of their plans to destroy an Order as well as to persuade the papacy that their proposal is the only logical outcome. Although the authority of the papacy was much weaker than in the previous centuries, and the present Pope Clement V attained his position by the help of the French monarchy, the papacy had the *de jure* authority in determining the culpability of a religious order, and at least for the record, a solid justification had to be provided. In short, the Parisian authorities needed to depict the Order as being atrociously detrimental to the Christian

---

[286] For example, this is evident in the response of the Grand Master of the Order, Jacobus de Molay, to Clement the V in G. Lizerand, *L'Affaire des Templiers* (Paris, 1923), pp.2-15.

welfare.

They did so by depicting the criminality of the Templars in terms of blasphemy, a common and serious category of criminality by the early fourteenth century. As Rufinus of Bologna commented on Gratian's *Decretum* in the latter half of the twelfth century, blasphemy, which placed one's mouth against the heaven, was a crime more horrible than any other crime. Its horrendousness was assumed in the very bedrock of Christianity,[287] since blasphemy attacked the central reason for its existence, God.

Although the text of Gratian's *Decretum* itself, which reflects a dexterity with biblical and exegetical sources, never explicitly defined blasphemy, it nevertheless provided some essential principles regarding blasphemy. It pinpointed that bad speech was evil regardless of a probing of the intent,[288] since the profanity presumed an evil intent; good speech, on the other hand, could actually be blasphemous based on a

---

[287] Rufinus von Bologna, *Summa decretorum [von] Rufinus of Bologna.* Ed. H. Singer (Paderborn, 1902), *ad* C. 23, q. 5, c. 6.

[288] *Decretum Magistri Gratiani*, 2d ed, ed. E. Friedberg, *Corpus Iuris Canonici*, I (Graz, 1959), C. 24, q. 3, c. 3 (*Qui non corde, sed ore maledicunt, labiorum inmundiciam contrahunt*) and C. 24, q. 3, c. 10 (*Ab omni maledicto fideles inmunes esse oportet*).

blasphemous intent; [289] furthermore, one's behavior and lifestyle may indicate the commission of blasphemy.[290]

The Bible, a significant source that ranked high in the range of authoritativeness in canon law, substantiated the definitions of blasphemy, both as speech and life. One committed blasphemy generally through speech of insult and ridicule of God, as Sennacherib king of the Assyrians did (II Kings 18: 19- 35) and God reprimanded such as blasphemy (II Kings 19: 22). The crucial determining factor was the intent, or the conditions of the heart of which the speech reflected. Blasphemy was disobedience to God's commands and a sin of defiance (Numbers 15, 30), [291] rebellion against God (Nehemiah 9, 18 and 26), and giving obeisance to things other than God, which is idolatry (Isaiah 66:3).[292]

---

[289] Ibid, C. 24, q. 3, d. p. c. 11: *Maledictum, quod prohibetur, est illud, quod procedit voto ultionis et odio persequentis, non ex amore iusticiae. Maledictum vero, quo sancti malediunt, est illud, quod procedit ex amore iusticiae, non ex livore vindictae.*
[290] Ibid, C. 3, q. 7, c. 7: *quorum vita cum esset blasphemabilis....*
[291] This includes sinning against God that makes *others* to show contempt for God (in the case of David's sin reprimanded by Nathan, II Samuel 12, 14.
[292] This notion is derived from comparing two translations, the Vulgate and the version quoted as used by Augustine in C. 1, q. 1, c. 98 where *qui benedicat idolo* (he who speaks well of an idol) is

Whether in word or in nonverbal expressions of the heart, blasphemy, whose object was God and whose prime characteristic was contumacious rebellion, was a serious sin. The case of Eli illustrates the seriousness of an offense when the object of the offense was God himself. Eli the priest in the Old Testament, when he heard about the evil things his sons were doing at the entrance to the Tent of Meeting, lamented that if a man sinned against another human being God may mediate for him, but if the object was God Himself, who will be the mediator (I Samuel 2, 25). The New Testament also states that blasphemy against the Holy Spirit is an unforgiveable sin.

The sin of blasphemy was thus a serious consideration in the centuries preceding the trial of the Templars, while witchcraft, although familiar to popular imagination and acquaintance with the occult, was not a serious category for criminalizing behavior in and of itself before the fourteenth century. C. 26 of the *Decretum* dealt with sorcery, it integrated the *canon episcopi* of earlier centuries, early writers, such as Isidore of Seville, treated astrology and other magical uses, and Aquinas discussed witchcraft. At most, however, superstition, misuse of creation, idolatry and worshipping of the devil were loosely connected together as witchcraft and denounced,

---

substituted for *blasphemus* (a blasphemer).

but not used as the political medium for destroying a group of people.

In fact, witchcraft was but an aspect of blasphemy. The centuries preceding the fifteenth century were bringing in different strands and elements that would make witch trials successful in later centuries. Blasphemy contributes to the development of the conceptualization of witchcraft.

On the other hand, the elements of blasphemy, which placed one's mouth against God through speech, intent, and attitude, are evident in the sources surroundding the trial of the Templars, from the depictions of a blasphemous group that led to the arrest to the intial round of depositions where lack of proper intent is invoked by the confessors to justify blasphemous acts.

It was, moreover, blasphemy, more than witchcraft, that framed the charges. The Templars were not depicted as witches engaged in the occult magical practices or in collusion with the devil; rather they were portrayed as disobedient, idolatrous and rebellious deviants of the faith whose blasphemous activities of the mouth (denying, spitting, kissing) reflected their blasphemous existence. The devil is mentioned in only very few cases and in a way that supports the intent element (fear that induced confession), and the kissing activity often associated with *maleficia* is significant in the very act of impurity rather than in the object of the devil, as in the case of witchcraft. Theirs is a case not of extraordinary superstition, but of a mundane situation where people were presumptious and contumacious.

More accurately, the trial indicates the casting of the members as blasphemers in a blasphemous organization that posed as a real danger in provoking God's anger, and if not eradicated would bring danger to the community. As such, Philip's plan to destroy the order and and the unrepentant members was not only an option but a necessity.

The immediate events and correspondences leading to the arrests, where the Parisian authorities bemoaned the infamy of the Order and members as a serious case of blasphemy, indicate the preliminary laying of the charges on principles of blasphemy. It was only then that the arresting of the Templars seemed the only logical step to take.

In one letter by a bishop to King James II in early fourteenth century, the writer indicated the offense in the existence of the Order of the Temple:

> *Iam vestre regie magestati nuper scripsisse recolimus graves iniurias et offensas, quas fratres Templi nobis et Ilerdensi ecclesie contra ius et iusticiam intulerunt.*[293]

---

[293] H. Finke, *Papsttum und Untergang des*

In the order of the arrest of the Templars on September 14, 1307, Philip of France detailed the heinousness of sins committed by the Order:

> *Res amara, res flebilis, res quidem cogitatu horribilis, auditu terribilis, detestabilis crimine, execrabilis scelere, abhominabilis opere, detestando flagicio, res penitus inhumana, immo ab omni humanitate seposita, dudum fide digna relatione multorum, non absque gravis stuporis impulsu et vehementis horroris fremitu, auribus nostris insonuit, cujus gravitate pensata eo crevit in nobis acerbius doloris immensitas quo talium et tantorum inmanitatem scelerum in divine majestatis offensam, orthodoxe fidei et tocius christianitatis dispendium, humanitatis obprobrium, exempli mali perniciem et generale scandalum, non est dubium redundare... Comparata est jumentis*

---

*Templeordens* (Muenster, 1907), vol 2, p. 6.

> *insipientibus, immo ipsorum insipienciam jumentorum stupenda bestialitate transcendens, ad illa omnium scelerum summe nepharia se exponit que abhorret et refugit ipsarum irrationabilium sensualitas bestiarum...*[294]

The order continued to detail their involvement with demons, insulting and denying Jesus Christ, horrible cruelty in spitting at the crucifix, immoral kissing, and idol worship.[295] After these descriptions, Philip lays out the reason for the arrest: for the defense of the ecclesiastical faith.[296] The concern for the honor of God and the firmness of the catholic faith,[297] which blasphemy attacked, was the motivating factor that Philip outlined. It is on this theme that Philip speaks in the Council of Tours in March 25, 1308, where he ends with the following:

> *Nos igitur ad extirpationem tantorum scelerum, tam gra-*

---

[294] Lizerand, pp.16-19.
[295] Ibid, pp. 20-21.
[296] Ibid, pp. 21-25.
[297] *Proces des Templiers*, ed. J. Michelet, vol I, *Collection de Documents Inedits sur l'Histoire de France* (Paris, 1841-51), p. 13: *ad Dei honorem et fidei catholice firmitatem.*

> *vium errorum, stabilitatem fidei necnon honorem sancte matris Ecclesie promovendum, ad sedem apostolicam conferre nos personaliter proponimus in proximo. Cujus operis sancti vos volumus esse participes, qui participes estis et fidelissimi zelatores fidei christiane;* [298] ...

A letter of Guillaume de Paris' letter, dated a week later on September 22 of 1307, which urges the Inquisitors of Toulouse and Carcassone to give their support in an investigation of the Templars, depicts the blasphemous nature of the Order:

> *Scelus sceleratissimum, celeste flagicium, quod nec oculus vidit nec auris audivit nec alias hominis cor ascendit: res amara, res flebilis, abhominabilis et nimis terribilis, ex qua consuevit ira Dei in filios difidencie provocari. Commovetur terra nimirum ac omnia elementa turbantur, divinum nomen contempnitur, religionis venustas confunditur, laceratur*

---

[298] Lizerand, pp. 106-107.

*stabilitas fidei christiane.*
....
*Heu nobis, si premissa veritate nitantur! Quis nobis, fratres, tribuat, ut tanti facinoris, tante divine <u>blasphemie</u> videamus aliquam ultionem.*
....
*Et si premissa scelera inveneritis esse vera, probis viris ordinis fratrum Minorum ac aliis religiosis viris negocium sic aperire curetis, quod apud eos vel populum non oriatur scandalum ex huiusmodi processibus sed odor pocius bone fame.*[299]

After the arrests of October 13, 1307, Philip the Fair wrote to King James II on October 16, 1307 and continued to detail the blasphemous nature of the Order:

*Licet autem ex talibus nobis ac patri sanctissimo summo pontifici, per se cuilibet nunciatis, ab inicio credere non possemus ullatenus, parvipendere tamen tantam Dei <u>blasphemiam</u> nimirum nolu-*

---

[299] Finke, II, pp. 44-46, underscoring mine.

> *imus, sed diligenter indagavimus veritatem, prefato sanctissimo patri summo pontifici Lugduni primo, secundo Pictavis negocio reserato nobis inquistore pravitatis heretice generali regni nostri, probis viris religiosis et aliis fide dignis adhibitis ac per testes fidedignos omni excepcione maiores heresis est predicta probata contra quamplures personas eius ordinis ac suspicio vehemens erroris eiusdem in omnes et singulos ordinis supradicti.*[300]

In Philip's letters to James preceding and during the first round of Paris depositions, Philip framed the issues to necessitate his conclusion and his perspective influenced James II as well.

According to James II to whom Philip had described the nature of the Templars, the Templars were enemies of the cross. He wrote to Philip the Fair on November 17, 1307, in the midst of the first round of depositions in Paris:

> *Excellencie vestre littere... non solum admiracionis*

---

[300] Ibid, pp. 46-47, underscoring mine.

> *causam set perturbacionis etiam prebuerunt eo potissime, quia dicti religiosi precessoribus nostris in exaltacione fidei et in inimicorum crucis depresssione labores non modicos cum effusione etiam sanguinis subire minime formidantes, mortis timore postposito, gratum et magnum servicium prebuerunt et multi ex eis mortem etiam incurrerunt...*[301]

Furthermore, King James II's letter to Pope Clement V at the end of 1307, December 29, after the Parisian authorities extracted 134 confessions, shows the casting of the Templars in the terms set by Philip the Fair:

> *si ordinem fratrum milicie Templi, qui pro destatabili crimine heresis vehementer suspecti sunt...*[302]

The framing of the case of the Templars as blasphemers by the French monarchy from the early stages of the trial, set the tone so that later defenses by the

---

[301] Ibid, p. 56.
[302] Ibid, p. 74.

Templars[303] about the nature of their confessions (forced under torture) did not attract attention. As far as the authorities were concerned, the confessions were voluntary: at the end of each of the 134 confessions included a statement that they made their confessions voluntarily. On October 26, 1307, Philip declared to James that *voluntate spontanea confitentur errores.*[304]

The Aragonese Inquisitor, Johannes de Lotgerio, reflected on the infamous nature of the Templars, on December 5, 1307, shortly after the end of the first round of depositions in Paris:

> *Dolentes deferimus set et certe vos ignorare putamus, quam vehemens et quam violenta contra vos et fratres vestri ordinis sit exorta de catholica fide suspicio et quam multipliciter de gravibus et sceleratis erroribus vos publica fama diffamet. Unde quia contra vos hec cotidie invalesci suspicio vehemencius et violencius fama clamat, iam ulterius hec sine Dei offensa, animarum periculo et scandalo plurimorum*

---

[303] Lizerand, pp. 176-189.
[304] Finke, II, p. 48.

*disimulare non possumus, set ex comisso nobis ab apostolica sede inquisicionis contra pestem heretice pravitatis officio urgemur descendere et inquirere cogimur, an invalescens suspicio et fama clamans huiusmodi opere sint complete...Significantes vobis ac predicentes aperte, quod ad exortam contra vos de catholica fide suspicionem non modicam presumpcionem adiceret, si citati ad respondendum de ea recusaretis contumaciter comparere.*[305]

In the course of the trial of the Templars, the authorities continued to focus on blasphemous nature of the members and the order so that the destruction of the Order, and not just the unrepentant members, would be an absolute necessity. For instance, in early 1308, Philip speaks about pertinacity and contumaciousness of the Templars as well as blasphemy against God to the masters of Paris:

*Sed occurit dubium ex eo quod, juxta legis divine preceptum, princeps secularis*

---

[305] Ibid, p. 68.

> *vel populus jurisdictionem exercens audit per hereticos vel scismaticos vel alios infideles nomen Domini <u>blasfemari</u> fidemque catholicam exsuflari...*[306]

Furthermore, the speech of Willelmi de Plaiano (Guillaume de Plaisians) on May 29, 1308 continues to depict the Templars as dangerous blasphemers:

> *Post illam universalem victoriam, quam ipse dominus Jhesus Christus fecit in ligno crucis contra [h]ostem antiquum pro defensione ecclesie sue et [h]umani generis redempcione... delegatos ad hoc in perfidorum Templariorum negocio, miraculose detegendo eorum pravitatem hereticam in animorum ipsorum periculum et subvertsionem fidei et destruccionem ec[c]lesie diucius occultatam... Fuit igitur dicta victoria in belli ingressu [h]orrenda et terribilis... not[oria] et indubitabilis... in[h]umanitatem criminum...*

---

[306] Lizerand, pp. 58-59, underscoring mine.

*[H]orrenda...*
*terribilis...propter*
*in[h]umanitatem criminum,*
*ex quibus, si vera erant, divina et humana subvertebatur natura... Ex predictis igitur necessarie concluditur predicta fore notoria et dilucida et indubitabilia, luce meridiana clariora, nec de cetero posse vel debere ab aliquo, qui sit verus catholicus et velit favoris heresis evitare periculum, in dubium revocari, nedum rebus manifestatis a Deo miraculose, ut predictum est, per dictum christianissimum principem et predictam Gallicanam ecclesiam, barones et omnes populos dicti regni...*[307]

In the next oration dated June 14, 1308, Guillaume continues to depict the Templars, as deviants of the faith who will cause the members of the body of Christ to fall and sin. Like heretics, they pervert the faith, so they must be amputated in order to save the whole.[308]

Accusations against the Templars in the order for their arrests issued by Philip

---

[307] Ibid, pp. 110-124.
[308] Ibid, pp. 124-137.

paralell the subsequent confessions of 134 Templars in the first round of depositions in Paris, October-November of 1307: 134 out of 138 confessed to various charges of the blasphemous uses of the mouth in abnegations, spitting, kissing, and lying. They particularly admitted to denying Christ and spitting on the crucifix, as well as engaging in the rite of kissing.[309]

The general format of the confessions starts with the name and identity of the brother, followed by the statement "*de tempore et modo sue recepcionis*" which introduces the time and mode of his recaption into the Order, such as where, when, and by whom. The set of confessions to the various charges is often preceded by "*dixit per juramentum.*" The substance of the confessions to acts of *spueret, abnegaret, osculum* (usually in that order but with variations) follows assertion of "*post multas promissiones de statutis et secretis dicti ordinis ab eo factas.*" Some confessions have reference to homosexuality withs statements such as *immiscuit se carnaliter*. The confessors often qualify their confessions to the charges and closes their confessions with a disclosure that they did not confess under torture.[310]

The act of denying articles of faith is

---

[309] Michelet, II, pp. 277-420.
[310] Ibid.

the most prominent aspect of their confessions, as a letter to King James II on February 19, 1308 from an Arnald von Villanova indicates:

> ... *Nam si reges fecerint hiis contraria, certum est, quod illa non agunt ut christiani sed ut de facto negantes Christum et eius religionem. Que abnegatio cum sit publica vel notoria, procul dubio magis est abominabilis in se ipsa, quam ea, que fit occulte, nec est minus stupenda quam illa, nisi pro eo, quia magis est assueta communi noticie. Supradicte vero apostasie christianorum notorie tanto sunt magis abominabiles, quanto maiorem <u>blasfemiam</u> et illusionem construunt adversus filium virginis, quoniam, qui predictis modis abnegant veritatem et sanctitatem sue religionis, eficatius movent infideles ad <u>blasfemandum</u> eum et ad respuendum, quecunque de ipso dicuntur et predicantur, racionabiliter arguentes vel argumentates, q uod, si talis et tantus esset Ihesus*

> *Nazarenus, qualem predicant christiani, non facerent universaliter et palam, quecunque illi contrariantur....Que <u>blasfemia</u> necnon illusio semper est in superioribus magis pestifera, quia trahit ad corrupcionem multipliciter subditos, inter quos ydiotas vel ignaros ad infidelitatem propellit.... Cum igitur abnegacio Christi, que fit oculte, constituat minorem eius <u>blasfemiam</u> et minorem universsitatis corrupcionem, constat, quod minus est dampnabilis apud Deum; set quia minus nota vel asueta, magis mirabilis et stupenda.*[311]

Another letter from Petrus of Lerida to King James II in early 1308 indicates that of the "acts" of the mouth, abnegation is the prime focus. The damnable acts of the Templars were first and foremost about denials of the essential articles of faith about God and the divinity of Christ:

> *... Est enim secretum Dei iudicium, ut tantarum Christi <u>bla[s]femiarum</u> magister, qui*

---

[311] Finke, II, pp. 95-96, underscoring mine.

> *tantis temporibus male vixit, tot alios ad sectam traxit dampnatam, remanere non debeat, quin ad exemplum in hoc seculo puniatur, nec enim sine scandalo facile posset ecclesia talis hominis misereri...*[312]

The abnegations provide the most poignant link with blasphemy, as the above letters indicate.

The letter of Petrus of Lerida, stated in part above, continues with a reference to one of the 134 confessors of late 1307 in Paris, Hugo de Paraudo, whose confessions is particularly vivid on the denials of Christ, which to Petrus are blasphemies, and the lack of intent to justify them:

> *et ipse tunc licet invitus Jhesum Christum abnegavit, ore, et non corde, ut dixit ...quod abnegarent crcifixum et crucem ter, et spuerent supra crucem et ymaginem Jhesu Christi; dicens quod, licet hoc eisdem preciperet, non faciebat corde...Dixit tamen quod non precipiebat eis predicta corde, sed ore solum.... Dixit tamen quod*

---

[312] Finke, II, p. 102, underscoring mine.

> *ore et fingendo adoraverat, et non corde: nescit tamen si alii fratres adorabant corde ...*[313]

Petrus' letter continues to emphasize the denials, which follow his reference to the blasphemies of Christ:

> *Professus abneget Christum: Respondeo, quod, licet iustus, ubi non vere dubitat, ad veritatem firmandam sepe per modum dubitacionis faciat questionem de ire certa tanquam de dubia, et hoc modo possit esse catholici questio supradicta, tamen, qui diceret talem professsionem tenere, quominus sit prorsus essencia vel substancia eius corrupta, vel qui vere super hoc dubitaret: non esset bene firmus in fide. Nam ut scriptum est: Dubius in fide infidelis est.... Primo propter profitentis errorem ...*[314]

The confession of Reginaldus pre-

---

[313] Michelet, II, pp. 362-63.
[314] Finke, II, p. 103.

ceptor domus Templi Aurelianensis contains an illustration of the denials to the essential points of a creed regarding Christ:

> *et quesivit ab eo per hec verba: Credis tu in eum? Et ipse qui loquitur respondit quod non; et statim quidam alius de fratribus predictis presentibus qui vocabatur Hugo, prout recolit dixit sibi hec verba: Tu bene dicis, quia ipse est unus falsus propheta. Et ipse qui loquitur intelligebat in corde suo, ut dicit, quod non credebat in ymaginem predictam, sed in eum cujus erat ymago predicta; et tunc quidam alius de dictis fratribus dixit dicto fratri qui sic locutus fuerat dicto recepto: Tace, tace; bene instruemus eum alias de statutis ordinis nostri. Et credit ipse qui loquitur quod dimiserunt tunc detegere sibi et eum instruere propter astantes circa capellam predictam et quia tarde erat et sic recesserunt.*[315]

The confessors qualify their con-

---

[315] Michelet, II, pp. 356-57.

fessions to the various charges by negating the element of intent behind the act more than the element of the act itself. Many of the 134 confessors repeat the formula, *ore sed non corde*, or its variants, to justify abnegations and spitting, blasphemous activities of the mouth that express disdain for God verbally and nonverbally.

In the confession of Gerardus de Gauche is the first occurrence of the distinction between the *ore* and the *corde*, with respect to a prior denial of the faith: *Et tunc ipse abnegavit ore, nunquam tamen abnegavit corde.*[316] The next occurrence, with the confession of Gaufridus de Charneio, is more specific about the object of the denial:

> *Et tunc fecit dictus recipiens ipsum abnegare Jhesum Christum ter, ore et non corde, ut dixit.*[317]

Another example that directly describes the object of the denials is in the confession of Matheus de Attrebato:

> *abnegaret Jhesus Christum, et spueret supra crucem... Et ipse tunc invitus, ore et non corde, Jhesum Christm ab-*

---

[316] Ibid, p. 291.
[317] Ibid, p. 295.

> *negavit, et finxit quod spueret ter supra crucem.*[318]

Michel de Fles is emphatic about the lack of intent in his denial: *nunquam negavit corde, ut dicit.*[319]

The negation of intent sometimes occurs with respect to the act of spitting. Johannes de Sancto Remino Suessionensis stated that *injunxit quod spueret ter super eam: quod fecit ore sed non corde, ut dixit.*[320]

In the 134 confessions of late 1307, the negation of intent also occurs simultaneously in two acitivities of the mouth: the denials and the spittings. Guillermus de Biceyo Lingonensis confessed:

> *quod abnegaret dictum Jhesus Christum, et ter spueret supra crucem, despiciendo Dominum Jhesus Christum qui passus fuit in ea; que fecit ore, et non corde, sicut dixit.*[321]

Richardus de Caprosia also confessed

> *et preceperunt ei quod*

---

[318] Ibid, p. 372.
[319] Ibid, p. 334.
[320] Ibid, p. 350.
[321] Ibid, p. 297.

> *abnegaret Deum cujus ymaginem videbat, et quod ter spueret supra crucem: que fecit ore, sed non corde, sicut dixit.*[322]

The close conjunction is especially noticeable in the confession of Guillermus de Herbleyo: *dictas abnegacionem et spuicionem ore fecit, licet non corde, sicut dixit.* [323] Hymbaudus de Laboyssade's qualification also shows that the activity described by the verb *facio* refers to the denying and the spitting: *abnegaret, et spueret...sed hoc non fecit corde, licet ore ut dixit.*[324]

The denyings and the spittings often occurred three times. Johannes de Basemont, for example, stated:

> *et tunc ipse qui loquitur negavit ter, et ter spuit supra crucem et ymaginem predictas, et hec fecit ore, sed non corde ut dixit.*[325]

Furthermore, Johannes de Amblanvilla said:

> *quod abnegaret ter eum, et*

---

[322] Ibid, p. 298.
[323] Ibid, p. 300.
[324] Ibid, p. 304.
[325] Ibid, p. 336.

> *ter spueret supra crucem ...,*
> *et tunc ipse qui loquitur*
> *negavit eum ter ore, sed non*
> *corde, ut dixit.*[326]

Although the denyings and the spittings on the cross normally occur three times, there are times when an act is done only once, as in the case of Petrus de Grumesnil Belvacensis: *Et tunc ipse abnegavit ter et spuit semel supra crucem, et ore tantum modo, et non corde.*[327] Petrus de Blesis also stated that *abnegavit semel ore, sed non corde, et spuit ter supra crucem.*[328] Ansellus de Rocheria also stated:

> *abnegaret eum ter, et ter*
> *spueret supra crucem....;*
> *quas abnegacionem et spui-*
> *cionem ipse fecit semel, ex*
> *ore, sed non corde, ut dicit.*[329]

Petrus de Monte Seudi's confession is another example:

> *Dixit eciam per juramentus*
> *suum quod per violenciam et*
> *contra voluntatem suam ab-*
> *negavit semel ore, et non*

---

[326] Ibid, p. 336.
[327] Ibid, p. 318.
[328] Ibid, p. 334.
[329] Ibid, p. 352.

> *corde, et non videtur sibi quod spueret supra crucem.*[330]

The case of Petrus de Monte Seudi presents another aspect of the confessors' recalling of the denounced act: *et <u>non videtur</u> sibi quod spueret supra crucem.*[331]

In the case of Radulphus de Bretencuria, he made a similar statement in the defect of consciousness:

> *abnegavit... et spuit ad terram, <u>fingens</u> se spuere supra crucem, et hoc fecit ore, sed non corde.*[332]

Johannes de Valle Bellaudi also stated:

> *abnegare... spueret...Sed noluit, imo spuit juxta eam, <u>fingens</u> quod supra eam spueret, et dixit quod abnegacionem hujusmodi fecit ore, et non corde.*[333]

Matheus de Attrebato also confessed:

> *abnegaret Jhesus Christum,*

---

[330] Ibid, p. 345.
[331] Ibid, p. 345, underscoring mine.
[332] Ibid, p. 337, underscoring mine.
[333] Ibid, p. 359, underscoring mine.

> *et spueret supra crucem... Et ipse tunc invitus, ore et non corde, Jhesum Christum abnegavit, et <u>finxit</u> quod spueret ter supra crucem.*[334]

Johannes de Anisiaco's confession contains another variation of the term:

> *abnegaret...spueret...et cum non vellet facere... et tunc ore, et non corde, abnegavit Jhesus Christum, et <u>simulavit</u> spuere supra crucem.*[335]

The case of Petrus de Monte Seudi also presents another dimension to the qualification of will: they also appeal to an imperfect will and action that is the result of coercion or necessity.

> *Dixit eciam per juramentus suum quod per violenciam et <u>contra voluntatem suam</u> abnegavit semel ore, et non corde, et non videtur sibi quod spueret supra crucem.*[336]

The acts were done *invitus* and *contra voluntatem* or out of fear (*metu, timore*

---

[334] Ibid, p. 372, underscoring mine.
[335] Ibid, p. 367, underscoring mine.
[336] Ibid, p. 345, underscoring mine.

*mortis*). Guillermus de Varnage qualified his confession with an imperfect will:

> *Qui licet <u>invitus</u> et turbatus ultra quam credibile esset... abnegavit...spuit... hoc faciens ut dicit, timore ipsorum; et de hoc tantum doluit et fuit turbatus...*[337]

Bernardus de Parisius likewise defended his actions with the qualification of *invitus*:

> *precepit sibi quod abnegaret illum cujus ymago representabatur ibi qui licet <u>invitus</u> abnegavit ore, licet non corde ut asserit immo doluit quantum potuit.*[338]

Other confessions are more detailed in the admissions to the charges qualified with the defense of a lack of will. In the case of the confession of Michael de Sancto Mannyo Ambianensis is the following:

> *Et recipiens adhuc sibi precepit in virtute obediencie, quod hoc faceret, et tunc ipse qui loquitur, licet <u>invitus</u>, ore, sed non corde, ut dicit, ter*

---

[337] Ibid, p. 302, underscoring mine.
[338] Ibid, p. 324, underscoring mine.

> *abnegavit eum, et ter spuit supra crucem et ymaginem predictam.*[339]

Adam de Monte Suessionis also stated:

> *et tunc ipse qui loquitur, licet <u>invitus</u>, ore, sed tamen non corde, ut dicit, abnegavit eum ter, et spuit ter supra crucem et ymaginem predictas ...*[340]

Robertus de Sarnaco Belvacensis admitted that *quod fecit ore, licet <u>invitus</u>, et non corde.*[341]

Johannes de Pruvino also stated:

> *faceret....abnegavit eum ter ore, et non corde, ut dicit, et spuit ter ad terram, sed non supra, quia hoc faciebat valde <u>invitus</u>, ut dicit.*[342]

Constancius de Biciaco la Coste admitted to a lack of will with another use of words:

> *Sed ipse <u>noluit</u> abnegare, nec*

---

[339] Ibid, p. 327, underscoring mine.
[340] Ibid, p. 328, underscoring mine.
[341] Ibid, p. 330, underscoring mine.
[342] Ibid, p. 355, underscoring mine.

> *predictam spuicionem fecit ex corde, ut dixit; et dixit per juramentum suum quod <u>ipse pocius voluisset</u> quod nunquam fuisset ordo Templi.*[343]

Similarly, Johannes de Valle Bellaudi stated:

> *abnegare... spueret...Sed <u>noluit</u>, imo spuit juxta eam, fingens quod supra eam spueret, et dixit quod abnegacionem hujusmodi fecit ore, et non corde.*[344]

Gaufridus de Fera also stated his lack of will twice: *sed ipse <u>non voluit</u> abnegare... sed <u>non voluit</u> spuere, immo spuit ad terram juxta crucem.*[345]

Statements referring to the actions out of fear further evidence the defense of an imperfect will. For instance, Guillermus de Chalou Regine stated that:

> *Et tunc ipse <u>metu mortis</u>, ut dixit per juramentum suum, abnegavit ter Jhesum Christum ore, sed non corde, ut dixit.*[346]

---

[343] Ibid, p. 351, underscoring mine.
[344] Ibid, p. 359, underscoring mine.
[345] Ibid, p. 389, underscoring mine.
[346] Ibid, p. 296, underscoring mine.

The confession of Odo de Wirmis Belvacensis contains a variant of this theme of acting out of fear:

> *quod abnegaret ter illum cujus ymago erat ibi, et ter spueret supra eam, <u>propter quod ipse fuit multum territus</u>, et finaliter ipse ore, sed non corde...*[347]

There are instances of presenting an imperfect act, when the confessors declare an uncompleted *actus reus* of spitting on the cross: one spitted *juxta* the cross,[348] and not on it, or on the ground: *spuere supra crucem, spuit <u>ad terram</u>*.[349] For instance, Petrus de Laigneville said: *fecit abnegacionem semel ore, et non corde, ut dixit... spuebat <u>ad terram</u>*.[350]

Even in these cases of negating the *actus reus* element of the charges, the confessors, in their efforts to justify their alleged abnegations and spittings on the cross, assumed that they committed the acts that the Parisian authorities attempted to classify as blasphemous. Such actions

---

[347] Ibid, p. 331, underscoring mine.
[348] Ibid, p. 109.
[349] Ibid, pp. 113, 114, 115-118, 121, 124-125, 131, 134-6, underscoring mine.
[350] Ibid, p. 415, underscoring mine.

committed in their part as members of the Order would provide sufficient and persuasive basis for destroying the Order. At the same time, the negation of the intent, will, or the significance of their acts would spare the individual confessors.

The first round of depositions in Paris, October and November of 1307 just after the first arrests on October 13, 1307, are significant because the confessions are elicited after a surprise set of arrests, and they further demonstrate the first phase of the trial of the Templars that sealed their fate. The letters of the authorities, whether French, English or papal, around this time demonstrate that particularly the French depicted the Templars as blasphemers worthy of nothing less than what they proposed: the destruction of the Order and the burning of the prominent members. The Templars were blasphemers in the most comprehensive meaning of the word: they used their mouths against heavens, which as pointed out earlier is an insight from Rufinus, in *various* ways, from denying Christ to spitting on the cross, as well as obscene kissing. The fact they the confessors tried to weaken the effects of their profane behavior by negating the intent also shows that the concerns of blasphemy, rather than witchcraft, were at the forefront, since intent is the determining factor in blasphemy as opposed to actions in the cases of witchcraft.

The thesis does not imply that the idea of witches as being dangerous was not serious enough or existing at the time. Rather, it implies that the sin of blasphemy was the bedrock underlying ecclesiastical apprehensions; that this concept is subtle and silent yet a significant aspect of criminalizing witchcraft later; that it also illuminates the role of *fama* both in criminal procedure (in *accusatio* as opposed to the *inquisitio* form) as well as in general; and that this ecclesiastical concern affected the secular realm as well. In fact, the case of Philip IV of France indicates how "spiritual" concerns of blasphemy permeated the secular realm, in form if not also in substance, and that the secular authorities were able to manipulate these ecclesiastical ideas for political ends.

# Understanding the History of Penance through Medieval Canon Law

This paper examines the interplay between canon law and penitentials particularly with respect to the ninth century condemnations of penitentials. This is significant since despite some similarities and even overlap, penitentials lacked a status that canon law had to claim for its legitimacy; yet penitentials survived conciliar and diocesan condemnations. The language of the conciliar condemnations and juxtaposition of penitentials and canon law reveal the underlying political and pastoral concerns related with penance. Furthermore, the relationship seemed mutual; each were both a source for and an influence on the other. After giving a background on penance and penitential, I will focus on the content of the ninth century condemnations and refer to selected portions of particular texts of penitentials. I will argue that the condemnations played a pivotal role in the transformation of penitentials. The language of these conciliar decrees encouraged a more explicit and clear reference to authority and other means of validating prescriptions in the penitentials. Penitentials started to look more like canon law collections, which addressed the administration of penance. Penitentials were not banned to extinction because of the condemnations, although the very process that kept them from disappearing contributed to a subtle change in the role of penitentials altogether.

## I. Background

The history of penance is a significant one. It involves the crux of Christianity: the repenting of sins and receiving of forgiveness through Jesus Christ. The terms "repentance" and "penance" differ in that the former refers to a universal concept referring to the state of mind that turns away from sin, while the latter is a more specific term referring to a specific act and formula in response to the commission of sin.[351]

From the period of the ancient church, penance was a means of disciplining and correcting Christians who sinned.[352] It

---

[351] Allen J. Frantzen, *The Literature of Penance in Anglo-Saxon England* (New Brunswick, New Jersey: Rutgers University Press, 1983), p. 12.

[352] John T. McNeill and Helena M. Gamer, *Medieval Handbooks of Penance: A translation of the principal libri poenitentiales and selections from related*

also had a sacramental aspect, "as a means of supernatural grace annulling the consequences of sin and recovering the favor of God."[353]

Penance was the "price of regaining his Saviour's favor" and the examining of faith as part of the penitent's confession. As Frantzen articulated it, "the priest asked the penitent about his beliefs as if he were a catechumen about to enter the Church."[354] Penitential activity was considered to have a life-giving, curative and healing power.[355] Through it, one had an intimate and personal encounter with God, God's forgiveness was rediscovered, and it restored personal sanctity.[356] It was one of the seven sacraments eventually affirmed by the Council of Trent.[357] In the beginning, the remedial measures of penance were public and unrepeatable. Exomologesis of confession and penance involved a process of public humiliation.[358] Administration of penance eventually became a private rite that was repeatable and contained no harsh

---

*documents* (New York: Columbia University Press, 1938), p. 6.
[353] McNeill and Gamer, p. 15.
[354] Frantzen, pp. 10-11.
[355] Hugh Connolly, *The Irish Penitentials and their significance for the sacrament of penance today* (Portland: Four Courts Press, 1995), p. 13.
[356] Connolly, pp. 15-17.
[357] McNeill and Gamer, p. 17.
[358] McNeill and Gamer, p. 8.

disabilities.[359]

Penitential books played an important role in this transformation of penance.[360] These handbooks marked a new method of penitential discipline, a new era in the history of penance.[361] Penitentials reflected and reinforced the developing practice of private penance for forgiveness of sins committed after baptism.[362] They placed an emphasis on the individual and his need to assume responsibility for his spiritual warfare.[363] It represented a move away from behavior that was spiritually harmful and toward healing from the effects of sin and instruction in virtues.[364] Penance was eventually dissociated from the assembled church, and there was no public exomologesis. Council of Toledo forbade the iteration of penance in 589, although earlier penitentials allowed or repeated practice. In 1215, the Fourth Lateran Council prescribed confession and penance as a universal obligation, for secrecy and at least once a year.

Penitentials were confessional manu-

---

[359] Pierre J. Payer, *Sex and the Penitentials: The Development of a Sexual Code 550-1150* (Toronto: University of Toronto Press, 1984), p. 7.
[360] McNeill and Gamer, p. 6.
[361] McNeill and Gamer, p. 23.
[362] Payer, p. 7.
[363] Frantzen, p. 13.
[364] Connolly, p. 21.

als that proliferated around the sixth to the twelfth century.[365] They were personal handbooks of reference for the priest-confessor in prescribing acts of atonement proper to the offenses.[366] They were designned as a self-contained text to guide every phase of the private penitential system, for the reception of the penitent by the priest to practical adjustments which enabled the sinner to perform the penance assigned to him.[367]

These penitentials had an effect on church discipline and social morality; they were codes, like criminal codes,[368] and they involved the problem of vicarious merit, sharing of merit, related to the rise of indulgences.[369]

The penitentials dealt with deadly sins, which in the first stage of the church included principal sins of idolatry, fornication and bloodshed. Hermes's category encompassed unbelief, incontinence, disobedience, deceit, sorrow, wickedness, wantonness, anger, falsehood, folly, backbiting, and hatred. Augustine included murder, adultery, impurity theft, fraud, and sacrilege in the category of "crimen". John Cassian came up with outlining of the eight vices as gluttony,

---

[365] Payer, p. 3.
[366] Payer, p. 9 and Frantzen, ix.
[367] Frantzen, pp. 17-18.
[368] McNeill and Gamer, p. 46.
[369] McNeill and Gamer, p. 48.

fornication, avarice, anger, dejection, languor, vainglory, and pride. Cassian exerted influence in the area of penitentials, since his students compiled most of the penitentials, and many of them arranged them according to the eight vices first systematized in Cassian's writings.[370]

Cassian also applied the principle of curing the vices by their contraries. This principle is apparent in many penitentials, including those of Columbanus and Cummean which were early Irish penitentials. Penitentials offered to the sinner the means of rehabilitation, and penalties included fasting and *superpositio* (special fast), vigils and cross vigil, flagellation (in Irish penitentials), monastic vow, deposing of rank, servitude, almsgiving (e.g. in Columbanus'), exile and pilgrimmage, and temporary exclusion from church.[371]

The significance of penitentials and the study of penitentials have been explored on different levels. Scholars like Lea, Oakley, and Tentler studied penitentials for a theory of social control. They saw the administration of penance in the penitentials as oppressive and punitive, as opposed to seeing them from the perspective of education.[372] Frantzen considered penitential by

---

[370] McNeill and Gamer, p. 19.
[371] McNeill and Gamer, p. 30.
[372] Frantzen, p. 2.

looking at the sacramental tradition to which they belonged.[373] Hence, "the long list of sins was less a mirror of society's evils than a schematic inventory compiled by clerics eager to ferret out every possible abuse."[374] A penitential reflected "a cleric's attempt to record typical penitential decisions for future reference - an attempt at standardization and uniformity."[375] For some, like Payer, the value of the manuals comes from the fact that because they were related to pastoral ministry, they reflected what people actually did to an extent,[376] and the penances contained in the manuals "are at least rough indicators of the perceived gravity of the various offenses."[377] Although the penitenttials may not reveal what actually happened or how the people perceived these administrations of penance, the penitentials reveal some aspect of medieval society and morality:

> On balance it seems unwarranted to claim that the audience of the handbooks was so small as to be unrepresentative of medieval morality. . . . [They] embrace the

---

[373] Frantzen, p. 4.
[374] Frantzen, p. 13.
[375] Frantzen, p. 13-14.
[376] Payer, p. 12.
[377] Payer, p. 13.

full range of medieval society.[378]

The study of penance is a complex one because it not only involves consideration of the history of penance and the role of penitentials, but also the transmission and recaption of penitentials, as well as influences of various penitentials on the practice of penance. The earliest penitentials were Celtic (Irish and Welsh) in origin. Irish penitentials reached Frankish lands by the late sixth century, although Frankish penitentials were prominent few centuries later. In Anglo-Saxon England, penitentials thrived by the late seventh, in Italy by the late eighth, and with the Spanish Visigoths in the beginning of the ninth century.[379]

According to Connolly, Irish, monastic church played a pivotal role in shaping the theology of penance. St. Patrick had found a church in Ireland in the fifth century. This church was monastic, in contrast to the continental one. Celtic monks had a moral concern for penitential exercises as a remedy for spiritual diseases that separated one from God, and individuals and groups of Christians had profound insights into the mystery of divine forgiveness.[380] The Irish church centered upon the monastery, as evident in

---

[378] Frantzen, pp. 15-16.
[379] McNeill and Gamer, p. 26.
[380] Connolly, p. 1-2.

the penitentials of Finnian (also spelled Vinnian), Columbanus, and Cummean.[381] This contributed to the significance of the Irish church in the development of penitentials, since the monastic church was "the locus theologicus out of which the penitential manuals were born,"[382] and monastic religion contributed to the rise of penitentials.[383]

The structure of Irish society, including petty kingdoms, nobleman's responsibility, law of custom on crimes and compensation, and pledge of item (honor price), was also significant in the development of Celtic penitentials. For example, determining the intentionality behind a particular act was a particular concern behind the law of custom on crimes and compensation, and "the Celtic penitentials were later to exhibit similar concern for determining the intentionality behind a particular act."[384]

The earliest penitentials were Irish: that of Finnian (ca. 525-50) is the earliest extant Irish penitential. This was "the first comprehensive, discriminatory and precise penitential produced in the Irish Church."[385] The penitential of Columbanus (600), compiled on the continent and depended on Finnians' wide sphere of influence in con-

---

[381] Connolly, p. 8.
[382] Connolly, pp. 9-10.
[383] McNeill and Gamer, p. 24.
[384] Connolly, pp. 3-4.
[385] Connolly, p. 32.

tinental Europe, was the earliest penitential used in continental Europe. Cassian's principle of *contraria contrariis curare* is clearly evident; other prominent elements are precision, attention to individuals, and an increase in the confessor-priest's role. Cummean (650) is another early Irish penitential, and this is the most comprehensive.[386]

Celtic penitentials introduced new methods of penance.[387] Irish penitentials represented "the first sharp break with the earliest form of penance known in the Church, a public ritual presided over by a bishop."[388] The Celtic penance also became "the typical penance of medieval Europe."[389] Ancient public penance was never established in England, and Theodore of Tarsus, the chief organizer of the English Church, adopted the essentials of the Celtic discipline.[390] English ones include that of Theodore of Canterbury (d. 690), Venerable Bede (d. 735), and Egbert of York (d. 766). Up to the ninth century, penitentials were valuable tools for pastoral ministry.

However, the creative, formative period of penitentials in the period prior to 813 was accompanied by problems of sources used in the penitentials and their

---

[386] Connolly, p. 33.
[387] McNeill and Gamer, p. 20.
[388] Frantzen, p. 5.
[389] McNeill and Gamer, p. 29.
[390] McNeill and Gamer, p. 26.

interpretations by the priest-confessors. The beginning of the ninth century marked the influence of Carolingian revival and intense ecclesiastical and canonical reform in the Frankish realm. Several church councils (Council of Chalons in 813 and Council of Paris in 829) and a diocesan statute in the ninth century condemned penitentials in the ninth century for their problematic authority and administration of penance. Following the condemnations, a new form of penitential literature appeared, exemplified in the penitentials of Halitgar of Cambrai (ca. 830) and Hrabanus Maurus (ca. 841-842) who wrote penitentials in a new key. Penitential canons came into ecclesiastical, liturgical, social and legal contexts in an unprecedented way. The practice of penance was affected by a new outlook on penitentials and a particular criterion for their validity. Such shift is significant, not so much in the short-term changes, but in the long-term consequences in the role of canon law and the practice of penance.

## II. Ninth Century Condemnations

With the privatization and localization in the administration of penances, problems arose with respect to administration and authority. Local priests, ignorant of canonical authority and lacking accountability to a higher authority, abused their powers. Public penance re-emerged with the reforms of Charlemagne.[391] Charlemagne called for "open sin, open confession," and penitentials were first condemned in the Council of Chalons in 813. The theme of " public penance for public crimes" continued in Mainz, 847.[392] Furthermore, confusion arose with the proliferation of penitentials, which were often contradictory. A new interest for canons and decretals had begun to awaken in Frankish monasteries since the preceding century.[393] This canonical activity affected penitentials negatively in that a huge number of penitentials often contradicted statements and canons of the Frankish synods.[394] As a result, ninth century councils, capitular collections, Pseudo-Isidorean decretals, diocesan statutes, "all point to what must be called an official ecclesiastical proscription in regard to the penitentials."[395]

Yet, confession in private was not attacked but generally supported. As

---

[391] Frantzen, p. 97.
[392] John T. McNeill. *Celtic Penitentials and their Influence on Continental Christianity*. (Paris: Librairie Ancienne Honore Champion, 1923), pp. 162-163.
[393] Hubert Mordek, "Kanonistische Activitaet in Gallien in der Ersten Haelfte des 8. Jahrhunderts," *Francia* 2 (1978) 19-25, p. 25.
[394] Mordek, pp. 20-21.
[395] Payer, p. 59.

Frantzen pointed out, "bishops did believe in private confession and penance." The Paris synod provided bishops to instruct the priests in inquiring discreetly according to canonical authority.[396] As Frantzen wrote,

> Their reservations against the penitentials were, therefore, not based on misgivings about private penance itself, and their support for public penance was not an attempt to reassert the older methods at the expense of the newer.[397]

There were dichotomous penitential systems in the ninth century continental churches.[398] It was not the act of confession and penance that was the real target for criticism but the safety of administration. These condemnations seemed to be "motivated by a genuine concern for the proper administration of penance."[399] Condemnations centered on the danger of opposition to canonical authority.

None of the councils held in 813 councils (Arles, Reims, Mainz, Chalons, and Tours) recommended the use of penitentials,

---

[396] Frantzen, p. 99.
[397] Frantzen, p. 100.
[398] Frantzen, p. 100.
[399] Payer, p. 58.

while Chalons condemned them. Theodulf, bishop of Orleans who influenced the condemnation and suggested that the priest should hear confession according to eight chief sins, proposed more structure behind administering penances, in contrast to existing penitentials which were impractical as guides for confessors.[400]

The issue of authority is crucial in the condemnation of penitentials at the Council of Chalons. The first canon begins with the confines of authoritative sources, and the second canon is replete with biblical citations. The first canon states:

> Decrevimus iuxta sanctorum canonum constitutionem et ceterarum sanctarum scripturarum doctrinam, ut episcopi assidui sint in lectione et scrutentur misteria verborum Dei, quibus in ecclesia doctrinae fulgore splendeant, et verborum Dei alimentis animas sibi subditas saciare non cessent. . . .[401]

Elsewhere, patristic authority of Augustine

---

[400] Frantzen, p. 99-103.
[401] MGH *Concilia* 1.274, c. 1.

from *De cura gerenda pro mortuis*[402] or Jerome on his comment on Paul's epistle to the Romans[403] are included. In canon 34, sacred canons, holy scriptures, and church customs are cited as basis of authority.[404] Canon 38 explicitly condemns penitentials on the basis of lacking proper basis of authority and hence containing certain errors:

> Modus autem paenitentiae peccata sua confitentibus aut per antiquorum canonum institutionem aut per sanctarum scripturarum auctoritatem aut per ecclesiasticam consuetudinem, sicut superius dictum est, imponi debet, repudiatis ac penitus eliminatis libellis, quos paenitentiales vocant, quorum sunt certi errores, incerti auctores, de quibus rite dici potest: Mortificabant animas, quae non moriebantur, et vivificabant animas, quae non vivebant; qui, dum pro peccatis gravibus leves quosdam et inusitatos im-

---

[402] MGH *Concilia* 1.281, c. 39.
[403] MGH *Concilia* 1.282, c. 45.
[404] MGH *Concilia* 1.280, c. 34: "quod in canonibus sacris invenerit aut quod illi secundum sanctrum scripturarum auctoritatem et ecclesiasticam consuetudinem rectius visum fuerit."

> ponunt paenitentiae modos, consuunt pulvillos secundum propheticum sermonem sub omni cubito manus et faciunt cervicalia sub capite universae aetatis ad capiendas animas.[405]

This canon provided that penances ought to be administered according to the ancient canons, the authority of Scripture, or ecclesiastical custom. Penitentials, on the other hand, contained errors and doubtful authorship. In the latter part of canon 38 contains another criticism of the use of penitentials: inappropriate administration of penances that do not fit the crimes.

The Council of Chalons addressed another issue of authority: that of the priests administering penances. It condemned the Scots for an irregular assumption of episcopal functions as well as priests who conducted private penance.[406] Confession in private *per se* was not attacked but supported;[407] canon 25 allowed for private penance as well as public penance, and canon 32 provided ways to aid the priests to

---

[405] MGH *Concilia* 1.281, c. 38.
[406] MGH *Concilia* 1.282, c. 42: "Sunt in quibusdam locis Scotti, qui se dicunt episcopos esse et multos neglegentes absque licentia dominorum suorum sive magistrorum presbyteros et diacones ordinant. . . ."
[407] MGH *Concilia* 1.280, c. 33.

administer confession. However, private penance was problematic where priests were incompetent. As canon 35 addressed, it was a cause of much grief that in the administration of penance, many expected not so much remission of sin but satisfaction of necessary time slots.[408]

The Council set limitations on the role of the clergy. Canon 46 prescribed discretion in the performance of other important ecclesiastical sacraments.[409] Canon 52 reiterated the theme of performing church duties with great religiosity and sanctity.[410] The emphasis that duties were performed before many (*coram pluribus*)[411] and before witnesses[412] attests to the conciliar concern for right administration by priests *secundum canonicam institutionem, sicuti iustum et rectum est*.[413] The guidance of the holy scriptures and the instituted canons[414] is crucial, as pointed out both in the beginning and the end of the Chalons canons.

---

[408] MGH *Concilia* 1.280, c. 35.
[409] MGH *Concilia* 1.283, c. 46: "In perceptione corporis et sanguinis dominici magna discretio adhibenda est. Cavendum est enim, ne, si nimium in longum differatur, ad perniciem animae pertineat . . . ."
[410] MGH *Concilia* 1.284, c. 52.
[411] MGH *Concilia* 1.284, c. 55.
[412] MGH *Concilia* 1.284, c. 56 and 1.285, c. 62.
[413] MGH *Concilia* 1.285, c. 64.
[414] MGH *Concilia* 1.285, c. 66.

Only one ninth-century diocesan statute of Rodulph of Bourges (c. 850) explicitly condemned the penitentials. Its section on condemnation comes directly from Chalons. Chapter 33 is a section *de modis poenitentiae vel remediis*,[415] which contains the exact text of canon 38 of Council of Chalons. The chapter contains further explication on the analogy with baptism: penance also purges sins just as baptism, martyrdom, almsgiving, forgiving others, preaching and good works, and charity. By these seven modes, the chapter goes on to conclude, remission is given and reward of eternal retribution acquired. This statute's condemnation of penitentials, in context, seems to be motivated not by condemnation of penance, but by concern for everyday practices of the people. Penance is one way to obtain remission of sin, and this ought not to be improperly administered according to faulty penitentials and incompetent priests.

In 829, the Council of Paris explicitly condemned the penitentials, providing concrete measures to bishops to search them out and to burn those they found. Chapter 32 indicated that penitentials were in opposition to canonical authority which warranted a complete abolition of the penitentials. This section criti-

---

[415] PL 119.719.

cized priests who, using penitentials, carelessly and ignorantly imposed penances contrary to the canon law prescription. Because these handbooks were opposed to canonical authority, they failed to cure the effects of sins and instead fostered them through flattery. This chapter prompted bishops to diligently find such booklets in their dioceses and burn them so that unskilled priests do not use them to the detriment of the people.[416]

The canons of the Council of Paris begins with a focus on what properly pertains to the Christian religion.[417] The doctrinal content is an important part of Christianity; hence, the issue of authority and sources is an indispensable and crucial consideration. A careless attribution or appropriation can lead to fatal errors and heretical ideas. The next chapter continues with doctrinal content that there is one universal church of God, the body whose head is Christ.[418]

Discussion of the nature of the church leads to the fifth chapter regarding the priests. It was their duty to admonish every single person in their parishes, so that each corrects himself and converts to God with whole heart, since iniquities cause

---

[416] MGH *Concilia* 2.633, c. 32.
[417] MGH *Concilia* 2.609, c. 1.
[418] MGH *Consilia* 2.610, c. 2.

imminent dangers. Furthermore, the life of the leader require that priests humbly subjected to the mercy of the Lord.[419] The next chapter mentions one way of cure from sin: through the sacrament of baptism,[420] and the following chapters expound on it. Focus on the actions of the priests and danger related to their position are explained in chapter 12.[421] The next chapter focuses on the priests' duty to beware of avarice,[422] and that in the matters of the church the bishops should hold a mode of discretion.[423]

Following the church canons is mandatory.[424] Church matters ought not to be done in a hasty manner[425] nor should the priests act out of envy rather than out of zeal for love.[426] Priestly conversation should be a testimony of a commendable life.[427] Bishops and other prelates, unless inevitable necessity impedes it, should guard their canonical hours especially with their clerics

---

[419] MGH *Concilia* 2.612, c. 5.
[420] MGH *Concilia* 2.614, c. 6.
[421] MGH *Concilia* 2.618, c. 12.
[422] MGH *Concilia* 2.619, c. 13.
[423] MGH *Concilia* 2.623, c. 16.
[424] MGH *Concilia* 2.624, c. 17: Quod nulli episcoporum liceat res ecclesiae extra constituta canonum passim in alterius iura transferre.
[425] MGH *Concilia* 2.624, c. 18.
[426] MGH *Concilia* 2.625, c. 19.
[427] MGH *Concilia* 2.626, c. 20: Ut conversatio sacerdotalis testes vitae probabilis habeat.

and discuss the holy scriptures daily.[428] The pastors are sent to the flock not so that they remember to conduct their own affair, but that of the Lord.[429] The prelates are to pay attention to the carnal and spiritual food of their subjects.[430] It is important that the bishops are not greedy, but hating avarice, they establish ministers for the sake of their parishes.[431]

As evident in the cited chapters of the council, much concern lay with the personal integrity, responsibility, respectability, and exemplary role of the ecclesiastical leaders. The respective duties and their confines of different ecclesiastical leaders composed an important topic.[432] Canonical authority[433] and the sacred canons[434] were important guidelines in clerical administration. All these consider-

---

[428] MGH *Concilia* 2.626, c. 21: Ut episcopi ceterique praelati, nisi id necessitas inevitabilis impedierit, maxime cum clericis suis horas canonicas custodiant et scripturas divinas cotidie....

[429] MGH *Concilia* 2.627, c. 23: Ut pastores gregem sibi commissum non ut proprium, sed ut dominicum tractare meminierint.

[430] MGH *Concilia* 2.628, c. 24: Ut praelati carnalem spiritalemque cibum sibi subiectis impendere studeant.

[431] MGH *Concilia* 2.628, c. 25: Ut episcopi non rapaces, sed avaritiam odientes vice sua ministros per parrochias suas constituant.

[432] MGH *Concilia* 2.630, c. 28- 2.633, c. 31.

[433] MGH *Concilia* 2.628, c. 26.

[434] MGH *Concilia* 2.629, c. 27.

ations preceded the condemnation of penitential handbooks in chapter 32.

The following is the language contained in chapter 32:

> Ut codicelli, quos penitentiales vocant, quia canonicae auctoritati refragantur, poenitus aboleantur. Quoniam multi sacerdotum partim incuria, partim ignorantia modum paenitentiae reatum suum confitentibus secus, quam iura canonica decernant, imponunt, utentes scilicet quibusdam codicellis contra canonicam auctoritatem scriptis, quos paenitentiales vocant, et ob id non vulnera peccatorum curant, sed potius foventes palpant, incidentes in illud propheticum: *Vae qui consuunt pulvillos sub omni cubito manus et faciunt cervicalia ad decipiendas animas,* omnibus nobis salubriter in commune visum est, ut unusquisque episcoporum in sua parroechia eosdem erroneos codicellos diligenter perquirat et inventos igni tradat, ne per eos ulterius

sacerdotes imperiti homines decipiant. Sacerdotes porro, qui aut muneris aut amorist aut timoris aut certe favoris causa tempora modumque paenitentiae ad libitum paenitentium indicunt, audiant, quid Dominus per Ezechielem prophetam terribiliter dicat: *Hec dicit dominus Deus: Quia locuti estis vana et viditis mendacium, ecce ego ad vos, ait dominus Deus; et erit manus mea super prophetas, qui vident vana et divinant mendacium; in consilio populi mei non erunt et in scriptura domus Israhel non scribentur nec in terram Israhel ingredientur; et scietis, quia ego dominus Deus. Eo quod deceperint populum meum dicentes: Pax et non est pax,* et post non multa: *Cum caperent animas populi mei, vivificabant animas eorum et violabant me ad populum meum propter pugillum ordei et fragmentum panis, ut interficerent animas, quae non moriuntur, et vivificarent animas, quae non vivunt, mentientes populo meo credenti mendaciis.* Praesbyteri etiam imperiti sollerti studio ab episcopis suis instruendi sunt, qualiter et confitentium peccata discrete inquirere eisque congruum modum secundum canonicam auctoritatem paenitentiae noverint imponere, quoniam hactenus eorum incuria et ignorantia multorum flagitia remanserunt impunita et hoc ad ruinam animarum pertinere dubium non est.[435]

This chapter beings by stating that the penitentials should be completely abolished because they are opposed to canonical authority, priests are incompetent in administrating penance, and hence penitentials are ineffective and even detrimental. Then this chapter goes on to criticize priests by comparing them to the false prophets condemned in Ezekiel 13:8-10, 18, 19. In this biblical passage, God condemns prophets who proclaimed false words and lying visions, who proclaimed peace when there was none, who ensnared the lives of the people and profaned God among God's people. What these leaders do in ignorance,

---

[435] MGH *Concilia* 2.633, c. 32.

carelessness or indiscretion is destructive of the spiritual welfare of the people to whom they minister.

Here, the focus is wider than the validity of authority of sources. It assumes the incompetence of local priests who were careless, ignorant and unskilled. These condemnations show concern for both the importance of authority and the proper administration of penance.

In effect, the condemnations did not eradicate the penitentials. It may have been an "official proscription" which led to an elimination from official ecclesiastical legislative documents, but in local levels, an effective enforcement against continued use was lacking. After the condemnations of Chalons and Paris, no councils or capitulary decrees recommended the use of penitentials.[436] In fact, in a late tenth century diocesan statute of Rather of Verona, there is an explicit *recommendation* of a penitential.[437] The action of the Council of Chalons 813 seems to have had little effect in prohibiting the use of penitentials. Even with the Paris Council of 829, which put up a more drastic fight,[438] the adopted methods failed.[439]

Furthermore, older penitentials con-

---

[436] Payer, p. 58.
[437] Payer, p. 59, note 23.
[438] McNeill, p. 163.
[439] McNeill, p. 167.

tinued to be copied in the ninth century. For example, the oldest manuscripts of the Irish penitentials of Columbanus and Cummean come from the second half of the ninth century. Finnian and *capitula iudiciorum* in a St. Gall manuscript come from the second quarter of the ninth century; the oldest manusript of the penitentials of Bede and Egbert come from the first third of the ninth century. Some were also still written in traditional styles and content in the ninth century, for example, St. Hubert Penitential, Penitential of Pseudo-Gregory, Penitential of Pseudo-Theodore, and Bede-Egbert Double Penitential. Furthermore, new kinds of penitentials came in: *Dacheriana* and *Quadripartitus* of the mid-ninth century.

The question is, why, despite the condemnations, were the penitentials still used? We need to look at this issue in terms of an evolution of penitential practice of four centuries in Celtic, monastic and papal church. Even with the condemnations, "currents favorable, in the main, to the system of the penitentials were setting strongly in."[440]

One important factor in the survival of penitentials and the significance they were able to play in canon law was the penitential written by Halitgar of Cambrai. It addressed the concerns expressed in the condemnations regarding the authority and competence of priests administering pen-

---

[440] McNeill, P. 167.

ances. In contrast to pre-condemnation penitentials, like the English penitential of Theodore, Halitgar's penitential satisfied the concerns of the reformers. It did so both in structure (first five books preceding the "Roman" penitential were organized like a canon law collection) and content (addressing the roles of priest-confessors and sanctity of practice). In this way, the ninth century condemnations, though seemingly ineffective, actually were extremely crucial in changing the practice of penance.

When the condemnations pointed out the lack of authority in earlier penitentials, it was apparently less about the act of citing authoritative sources than the method of presentation and provisions ensuring the validity of sources, respectability of the practice, and soundness of administration. Theodore's penitential, before the condemnations, for example, included citation and reference to many authorities. The penitential seemed to be the product of an attempt to compile different texts. But the crux of the reformers' concern lay with administration and the authority of those administering the penances.

## III. Penitentials: Pre- and Post- Condemnations

I will focus on the penitential of Halitgar of Cambrai and that of Theodore of

Canterbury in light of intermediary conciliar condemnation. The former was written in 830 after the Paris condemnation. It is comprised of six books, the first five of which is modeled after canon law, and the sixth one which is claimed to be a "Roman" penitential. I will compare and contrast it to Theodore's penitential of the seventh century, written before the ninth century conciliar condemnations. This penitential was used as a source for other penitentials as well as the *Hibernensis*, which is a canon law collection of the eighth century, which, unlike other canon law texts, used patristic sources and included penitential sources.

In 830, Halitgar, at the request of Archbishop Ebbo of Rheims, wrote the penitential. It was written to address the concerns of the reformers who attacked the penitential handbooks. Halitgar's version provided for *ordo confessionis*, included private and public confessions, and brought it into alignment with canon law.[441] After Halitgar's efforts, penitential as a text was accepted in Rome and elsewhere as a standard guide to private confession and penance.[442]

The earlier penitential of Theodore of Tarsus,[443] archbishop of Canterbury, was comprised around 668 to 690. It was so

---

[441] Frantzen, pp. 103-104.
[442] Frantzen, p. 104.
[443] McNeill and Gamer, pp. 179-215.

influential that not only the canon law collections such as the *Collectio Hibernensis* utilized it, but also "half a century later Raban Maur at least twice cited the penitential canons of Theodore"[444] in his penitential. This penitential was not a direct work of Theodore. Rather,

> It professes to be made up mainly of answers given by the archbishop to a certain presbyter, Eoda, and edited, after a period of circulation in a confused state, by a scribe who hides behind the vague pseudonym "Discipulus Umbrensium."[445]

It seems evident that the penitential was prepared "by a person or persons familiar with Welsh and Irish penitential documents."[446] It used an Irish booklet as a source.[447]

*Collectio Canonum Hibernensis*,[448] a canon law collection, drew source from this penitential. This was an Irish collection "written for the early Irish church, [and] reflective of traditions and institutions of

---

[444] McNeill and Gamer, p. 179.
[445] McNeill and Gamer, p. 180.
[446] McNeill and Gamer, p. 181.
[447] McNeill and Gamer, p. 183.
[448] McNeill and Gamer, pp. 139-142.

little or no relevance to either Frankish or English ecclesiastical legislation."[449] Decrees and canons of Irish synods were incorporated into the compilation,[450] and it itself had Irish penitential texts within it.[451] Sheehy explains the apparent contradictions in the compilation as being caused by the existence of two factions in the Church: one slavishly imitating Roman practice and the other acknowledging the social polity of Irish tribal, rural society where the social and economic unit was the kin or family.

Although the Irish influences are significant in the penitential traditions and in the development of early canon law, the ninth century condemnation of penitentials was directed at the Irish tradition and strands in the penitentials. Reynolds points out that "Irish penitential discipline was vigorously attacked in the Carolingian period, and the books that contained this discipline, the penitentials, were condemned by several

---

[449] Frantzen, p. 129.
[450] Maurice Sheehy, "Influences of Ancient Irish Law on the Collectio Canonum Hibernensis," *Proceedings of the Third International Congress of Medieval Canon Law*, ed. Stephan Kuttner, Monumenta iuris canonici, Ser. C, Subsidia 4 (Citta del Vaticano: Biblioteca Apostolica Vaticana, 1968), 31-42, p. 31.
[451] Roger E. Reynolds, "Unity and Diversity in Carolingian Canon Law Collections: The Case of the *Collectio Hibernensis* and Its Derivatives," *Carolingian Essays*, ed. Uta-Renate Blumenthal (Washington, D.C.: The Catholic University of America Press, 1983), 99-136, p. 102.

early ninth-century councils."[452]

Yet, the Irish collection, *Hibernensis*, is significant on several levels. On one level, it was the only canon law collection at that time that used penitentials as its sources. On another level, it was a manuscript that was more essential than any until now in the eighth century because it offered the Frankish Reformers numerous patristic materials and areas of agreement between Irish and Roman rights and provided a surfeit of information on actual questions of church life.[453] It was also "the first text which reflects a coming together of ecclesiastical and secular law."[454] Despite Carolingian rulers' disapproval of the Irish texts, "the *Hibernensis* continued to flourish and luxuriate in a variety of contexts both canonical and literary as well as geographical."[455] It is sprinkled throughout penitential literatures and has become a source of biblical and patristic citations. In fact, despite Charlemagne's reform to have a "Roman" collection, what he espoused was actually Frankish and Irish:

> the Carolingian canonistic complex contained not only

---

[452] Reynolds, p. 102.
[453] Hubert Mordek, "Kanonistische Activitaet in Gallien in der Ersten Haelfte des 8. Jahrhunderts," *Francia* 2 (1978), 19-25, p. 20.
[454] Frantzen, p. 41.
[455] Reynolds, p. 133.

Roman and Frankish elements, but a strong Irish component in the *Collectio Hibernensis* and its derivatives.[456]

Reynolds points out the manuscripts and editions of the *Hibernensis*. There are two types: a shorter (A) version and a longer (B) version, written in St. Gall and Celtic Brittany, respectively.[457] There are seven manuscripts containing abridgements of the *Hibernensis*[458] and it has acted as supplements to other canon law collections, for instance the *Collectio Sangermanensis*, *Collectio Vetus Gallica*, and Collection of Bonneval.[459]

*Hibernensis* was most likely compiled by two monks, Rubin of Dair Inis (d. 725) and Cuchuimne of Iona (d. 741) and dated around the first quarter of the eighth century. McNeill and Gamer point out that it resembles little of penitential books in its nature and characteristics, although book 47 is titled "*De penitentia*" with twenty capitula including non-Irish sources. Furthermore, there are various isolated extracts of the work portions that belonged to the medieval penitential literature, particularly those that

---

[456] Reynolds, p. 101.
[457] Reynolds, p. 103.
[458] Reynolds, pp. 104-108.
[459] Reynolds, pp. 108-114.

"vary widely from earlier parallels or are found in their earliest known form in the *Collectio*."[460] Its sources of authority include Irish synods, Roman treatises, and writings of St. Patrick. The content encompasses topics such as priest's absence, consequences for homicide, monastery rule for seven years as a penance for intentional killing, theft in a Church and the role of priests' discretion; it also covers consequences for stealing in a church (a severe cutting of hand or foot or prison for fast, or pilgrimage and becoming a monk), for railing against a good prince, and for deserting infants.[461]

Canon law collections had little allowance for private penance, although the *Hibernensis* and the *Vetus Gallica* used Theodore's penitential as a source. *Hibernensis* four times quoted Theodore's penitential.[462] The canons were from earlier synodical decisions, patristic sources and papal decretals; they did not assign penances nor intended to be used by the confessor but to aid bishops and archbishops in maintaining ecclesiastical discipline on a broader scale.[463]

A comparison of Theodore's penitential, which was used as a source of

---

[460] McNeill and Gamer, p. 139.
[461] McNeill and Gamer, pp. 140-142.
[462] McNeill and Gamer, p. 181.
[463] Frantzen, p. 99.

*Hibernensis*, an Irish canon law collection, and Halitgar's penitential will enlighten the effects of the 813 condemnations that directly led to the writing of Halitgar's penitential. It reveals the central part that the condemnations played in the eventual transformation of the penitentials. Theodore's penitential was not oblivious to the need to cite authority and concerns to prevent confusion from sloppy writing. Yet, Halitgar's version differed from prior penitentials in ways that satisfied the concerns of the reformers.

On the one hand, Theodore's penitential also contains elements that seem to satisfactorily address the concerns expressed in the condemnations. It begins with this pastoral concern behind the writing of the Penitential:

> beloved, from love of your blessedness, I thought it fitting, to set forth whence I have collected the penitential remedies which follow, in order that the law may not, on account of the age or negligence of copyists, be perpetuated in a confused and corrupted state, as is usual.[464]

---

[464] McNeill and Gamer, p. 182. Subsequent cites and references of Theodore's penitential come from McNeill and Gamer's edition, pp. 182-215.

Not only is there a consciousness of the need to prevent confusion in the handbooks, but also of the importance of authority. The penitential from the start begins with many scriptural references. In fact, the law of penance is stated as having been proclaimed by Jesus Himself "when he was baptized before us all, proclaimed as the instrument of his teaching for those who had no means of healing; saying: 'Do penance,' etc." Besides this reference to Matthew 4:17 are also references to Matthew 18:18 ("Whatsoever thou shalt loose on earth shall be loosed also in heaven,") and Acts 20:24 ("for I have received of the Lord"). Furthermore, there are other signs of reliance on and mention of ecclesiastical and patristic authority: Gregory Nazianzen, Roman Church custom, Dionysius the Areopagite, and Augustine. The epilogue also contains the stamp of authority:

> Our [authors], as we said, have written these [canons] in consultation with the venerable Theodore, archbishop of the English.

For instance in the prescriptions against fornication, there is a reference to what Basil says regarding habitual sexual offenses. This is also an instance of the inclusion of a canon in the penitential. Furthermore, the canons of Theodore's penitential are directed at the clergy in particular.

On the other hand, upon a closer observation and comparison of Theodore's penitential, which was before the ninth century condemnations, and Halitgar's penitential, which was compiled in response to the condemnations, there are significant differences. Halitgar's penitential, unlike Theodore's, addresses the Carolingian insecurity for a "Roman" text. The sixth book of Halitgar's work is referred to as a *Roman* penitential. This sixth book is the focus of our inquiry and is comparable with Theodore's penitential. Halitgar's penitential also starts with various liturgical provisions that add sanctity and respectability to the administering of penance. It further focuses on the life, behavior, role and integrity of the clergy. It gives more specific and simpler directions to priest-confessors for administering penances and emphasizes the molding of their character in everyday life so that they are worthy and capable as priest-confessors.

In contrast to Theodore's penitential, the beginning of Halitgar's "Roman" penitential[465] prescribes several prayers that a priest is to recite before administering penances: "When therefore, anyone comes

---

[465] Cites and references of Halitgar's penitential come from McNeill and Gamer's edition, pp. 297-314.

to a priest to confess his sins, the priest shall advise him to wait a little, while he enters into his chamber to pray. But if he has not a chamber, still the priest shall say in his heart this prayer." And the penitential presents a long prayer:

> Lord God Almighty, be Thou propitious unto me a sinner, that I may be able worthily to give thanks unto Thee, who through Thy mercy hast made me, though unworthy, a minister, by the sacerdotal office, and appointed me, though slight and lowly, an intermediary to pray and intercede before our Lord Jesus Christ for sinners and for those returning to penance. And therefore our Governor and lord, who will have all men to be saved and to come to the knowledge of the truth, who desirest not the death of the sinner but that he should be converted and live, accept my prayer, which I pour forth before the face of Thy Clemency, for Thy menservants and maidservants who have come to penance. Through our Lord Jesus

Christ.

The act of administering really begins with the priests's confession of his own sins. This prepares the priests to act in humility and caution in administering the penance, since it was by God's mercy that he is acting as an intermediary. The whole process further emphasizes a restorative and reforming purpose of penance, rather than punitive.

When the administration of penance begins, the priest shall recite from the book of Psalm: "Rebuke me not O Lord in thy indignation" (Psalm 37). Then he leads the prayer with Psalm 102:5, beginning with "Bless the Lord O my soul" and ending with "shall be renewed." After saying "Let us pray" again, the priest shall recite Psalm 50:3-11. Then he is to recite Psalm 63 and Psalm 51:3-8 after saying "let us pray for the third time. In the fourth "Let us pray", the priest shall say the following four preliminary prayers:

> (1) O God of whose favor none is without need, remember, O Lord, this Thy servant who is laid bare in the weakness of a transient and earthly body. We seek that Thou give pardon to the

confessant, spare the suppliant, and that we who according to our own merit are to blame may be saved by the compassion through our Lord Jesus Christ.

(2) O God, beneath Whose eyes every heart trembles and all consciences are afraid, be favorable to the complaints of all and heal the wounds of everyone, that just as none of us is free from guilt, so none may be a stranger to pardon, through our Lord Jesus Christ.

(3) O God of infinite mercy and immeasurable truth, deal graciously with our iniquities and heal all the languors of our souls, that laying hold of the remission which springs from Thy compassion, we may ever rejoice in Thy blessing. Through our Lord Jesus Christ.

(4) I beseech, O Lord, the majesty of thy kindness and mercy that Thou wilt deign to accord pardon to this Thy

servant as he confesses his sins and evil deeds, and remit the guilt of his past offenses – Thou who did'st carry back the lost sheep upon Thy shoulders and did'st hearken with approval to the prayers of the publican when he confessed. Wilt Thou also, o Lord, deal graciously with this Thy servant; be Thou favorable to his prayers, that he may abide in the grace of confession, that his weeping and supplication may quickly obtain Thy enduring mercy, and, readmitted to the holy altars and sacraments, may he again be made a partaker in the hope of eternal life and heavenly glory. Through our Lord Jesus Christ.

These prayers are reminiscent of the fact of human weakness and the need of Christ's mercy to cure the souls. This weakness pertains not only to the present penitent but also to all, including the priest-confessor.

The fifth prayer is that of the imposition of hands which also appeals to God the Father for the healing of spiritual wounds through His Son and for pardoning the one who has fallen. Furthermore, this prayer asks for His mercy help in persevering until the end:

> Holy Lord, Father Omnipotent, Eternal God, Who through Thy son Jesus Christ our Lord hast deigned to heal our wounds, Thee we Thy lowly priests as suppliants ask and entreat that Thou wilt eign to incline the ear of thy mercy and remit every offense and forgive all the sins of this Thy servant and give unto him pardon in exchange for his afflictions, joy for sorrow, life for death. He has fallen from the celestial height, and trusting in Thy mercy, may he be found worthy to persevere by thy rewards unto good peace and unto the heavenly places unto life eternal. Through our Lord Jesus Christ.

This prayer continues to emphasize humility of the priests who should realize their own sins and tendency to err. That they are mere suppliants and not infallible would alert a priest to be cautious in their administrations. Following this prayer begins the Reconciliation of the Penitent on Holy Thursday, first with the recitation of Psalm 50 and antiphon "Cor mundum," followed by four more prayers:

> (1) Most gracious God, the Author of the human race and its most merciful Corrector, Who even in the reconciliation of the fallen willest that I, who first of all need Thy mercy should serve in the workings of Thy grace through the priestly ministry, as the merit of the suppliant vanisheth may the mercy of the Redeemer become the more marvelous. Through our Lord Jesus Christ.

It is God who corrects, not the priest who is merely performing his duty before God. In fact, the priest realizes his need of God's mercy most of all.

> (2) Almighty, everlasting God, in Thy compassion relieve this Thy confessing servant of his sins, that the accusation of conscience may hurt him no more unto punishment than the grace of

> Thy love [may admit him] to pardon. Through our Lord Jesus Christ.

This prayer recognizes that the focus of these penances is not so much physical suffering by penances nor the administration of penances, for the sake of their rigor, but rather the restoration and relief of the pained conscience through this administration of penances, which is original spirit of penance.

> (3) Almighty and merciful God, Who hast set the pardon of sins in prompt confession, succor the fallen, have mercy upon those who have confessed, that what is bound by the chain of things accursed, the greatness of Thy love may release.

The focus is continually the spiritual, the thing that matters most—more than the physical penances and the intricacies of it all, as has been the case in penitentials preceding the condemnations, as evident even in Theodore's penitential.

> (4) O God, Who gavest to

> Thy servant Hezekiah an extension of life of fifteen years, so also may Thy greatness raise up Thy servant from the bed of sickness unto health. Through our Lord Jesus Christ.

The emphasis of this last prayer regards the restoration from (spiritual) illness to (spiritual) health. The sins committed rendered the penitent spiritually ill and his confession, like Hezekiah's prayer to God, bestows on him blessing. It is after this whole litany of prayers and scriptural recitations that the prescriptions of penance begins.

Halitgar's penitential's focus on the cure of the soul contrasts Theodore's penitential whose main purpose of compilation was clarity and proper transmission to future generations:

> I thought it fitting, to set forth whence I have collected the penitential remedies which flow, in order that the law may not, on account of the age or negligence of copyists, be perpetuated in a confused and corrupted state, as is

> usual – that law which of old time God gave figuratively by its first promulgator and then later committed to the Fathers, that they should make it known to their sons that another generation should be acquainted with it. . . .

While the content of Halitgar's penitential affirmatively proved its authoritative nature by its grasp of the true spirit of penance, Theodore's penitential was apologetic -- it attempted to defend the rightness of its intentions ("For in all these things equally and without invidious discrimination according as I am able") and its methods ("I carefully select out of the whole the more useful things I have been able to find, and I have collected them, prefixing headings to them one by one"). Although Theodore's penitential mentioned that the compilation was done "for the sake of that kingdom of which He preached," it lacked content substantiating and demonstrating how exactly the penitential achieved the goal.

Besides the prayers, Halitgar's penitential clarifies from the outset the duties of the priest-confessors who partakes in this spiritual restoration. They are to also "unite with [the penitents] in fasting for one or two weeks, or as long as [they] are able."

Their role was not that of some tyrant or hypocrite against whom Jesus said, "woe unto you scribes, who oppress men, and lay upon their shoulders heavy loads, but ye yourselves do not touch these burdens with one of your fingers" but of someone who bends down and helps with his hand, of physicians who come in contact with the foulness of their patients. Such role requires the priests to live a life of "intense solicitude and the prayer of tears" and be in a position of helping when another member of the body is suffering. Hence, "the bishops or presbyters ought to humble themselves and pray with moaning and tears of sadness, not only for their own faults, but also for those of all Christians." The priests are to be actively participant in acknowledging their own sins, partaking in penances, and feeling the weakness of the penitents. The prologue to the sixth book includes II Corinthians 11:29: "Who is weak and I am not weak; who is scandalized and I am not on fire."

After the prologue, the prescriptions of penance begins with various sins and corresponding penances. Halitgar's penitental remains true to its spirit in focusing on the cure of the souls. The penances are not complicated and detailed, as with Theodore's. In the first section on homicide (1-5), Halitgar's prescriptions, though not simplistic, are simpler and more easily administratable. The main distinctions in penances pertain to the agent (commission by a bishop or any ordained person as opposed to a layman) and the the nature of the act (with consent, intent, and overlaying of infant). In c. 79-80, Halitgar deals with additional nuances of homicide involving alleviating and justificatory factors. Killing a man in a public expedition without cause demands relatively a lighter penance, and killing accidentally in self-defense or in defense of one's parents or one's household justifies the act of killing. The actor nevertheless may fast if he desires. On the other hand, if someone kills a victim without an alleviating or justifying condition, at a time of peace and for the purpose of taking the victim's property, the actor shall perform penance for a longer period and further shall restore the property to the slain man's family.

In contrast, the penitential ascribed to Theodore contains finer distinctions. Under the discussion of manslaughter (Book One, IV), penances differ according to revenge of whom (relative or brother) for which the slaying occurred and according to the identity of the victim (monk or a cleric versus bishop or presbyter). With respect to slaying a man in revenge of a relative, penance is lighter by half if the penitent gives a legal price to the relatives, and with respect to the slaying of a man in revenge of a brother, penance is either three years or ten years. Theodore also includes cases in which one kills with malice aforethought and distinguishes among killing through anger, by accident, by a potion or any trick, or as a result of a quarrel (which warrants the most years of penance). Although Theodore's penitential also includes some of the same things that Halitgar's penitential includes later (killing under command or public war, or by accident), Halitgar's penitential organizes provisions in a way that is simpler for administration.

On fornication (6-21), Halitgar prioritizes the penances for clergy which includes the priest-confessors. Halitgar differentiates penances between a cleric and a layman in certain circumstances and focuses on the former quite extensively. Halitgar first targets this group in addressing the commission of adultery and begetting of a child with the wife or the betrothed of another and then further addresses a cleric who repeats this offense. He includes a provision addressing a cleric who lusts after a woman and a cleric who returns to secular habit or takes a wife. After discussion of clerical abuses, this section on fornication goes on to consider penances for others, whose penances are lighter.

Theodore's penitential is also more cumbersome in detail. It includes more specific situations, such as fornication with mother and sister. Penance for committing fornication with a married woman entails a complex formula: penance for four years, two of these entire, and in the other two during the three forty-day periods and three days a week. There is another penance that gives the option of doing penance for one year or three forty-day periods. Different options of penance (forty or twenty days) gives more discretion to the administrators. C. 14 provides that if a woman who commits fornication has a husband, the penance is "greater" but none is specified. In the next clause, penance is prescribed as seven years, to the end of life or twelve years. Fornication with mother has penance of fifteen years without changing except on Sundays, or seven years with perpetual pilgrimage. This penitential accounts for various penances, without clearer guidance for administration, which leaves the priests with great discretion.

Regarding perjury (22-25), Halitgar continues to prescribe different penances for a cleric versus a layman (the clergy have heavier penances) and his distinctions, once again, are simple. Halitgar focuses on situations of necessity, ignorance, and act of cupidity. Normally, the penitents must to penance for three years and also render a life by releasing a slave from servitude or giving alms liberally. Perjury committed through cupidity, however, will be counteracted by selling all property, giving to the poor, and entering a monastery until death.

On the other hand, Theodore's treatment of perjury (Book One, VI) includes a fine point: committing perjury *in a church* leads to penance for eleven years as opposed to the normal three years. At the same time, there is no consideration of different states of mind (cupidity versus ignorance) as in Halitgar's penitential. Theodore also includes a provision distinguishing the swearing on the hand of a bishop or of a presbyter or of a deacon or on an altar or on a consecrated cross and lying (three years of penance) and swearing on an unconsecrated cross (one year) without providing for the penances of clergy in particular. Halitgar's penitential is also practical in being more specific on the nature of penance as well as on the connection between sin and remedy.

Of theft, Halitgar (in 26-30) continues to differentiate between a cleric and a layman, as well as apply principle of contraries for a layman who commits theft. If this person cannot restore what he had stolen, he must to penance and give alms to the poor from the product of his labor. Thedore's provisions (Book One, III), on the other hand, demonstrates a preoccupation with offenses against monks and churches. For example, a layman who carries off a monk from the monastery by stealth is noted, and money stolen from churches are restored for two times more than money from secular persons, and a special penance is required for one who has stolen consecrated things. There is no effort of restraining thieving by clergy; in fact, Theodore gives priests discretion to determine a sentence for others who often committed theft.

In comparison with Theodore's penitential, Halitgar's penitential is more confident. It is less apologetic about its compilation, it outlines a clearer delineation of canon law, and it boldly exhorts and admonishes clergy. It also carries an aura of *gravitas*, exemplified by the liturgical format prescribed by the penitential. In addition to respectability and authoritativeness that such sanctity confers in more realistic and convincing way than by mere quotation of sources, Halitgar's penitential is practical. The liturgical aspect renders the exercises more relevant, clear directions to confessors that address and alleviate problems caused by irresponsible and careless ministers make the penitential more credible, and discussion and categories simple in distinctions yet adequate in detail deems it administratable by clergy.

Halitgar's penitential epitomizes and represents the first of its kind. Increasingly the penitentials that contained the administering of penances had to take the form and tone reminiscent of canon law collections. As a result of the ninth century condemnations and Halitgar's response specifically to these condemnations, it became less useful to have the traditional penitential books. In time canon law collections would include sections on penance. Furthermore, the consciousness raised in the ninth century condemnations regarding the discipline of clerics, validity of sources, and legitimation of ecclesiastical practices would find its way in canon law collections in general.

Subsequent to the condemnations was an increasingly more consciousness of canonicity and authority of sources and administration of penance. This in turn effected the prominence of canon law in its treatment of penance. Although prior to the condemnations, penitentials influenced canon law by its inclusion as a source in canon law collections, the condemnations ushered in the next stage in the development of penance: a legalization and legitimation of a pastoral ministry and communal practice.

In the end, Halitgar's penitential after the ninth century condemnations was a product of a transformation of penitential exercises. Along the path were influences of canon law on penitentials and penitentials on canon law. With Halitgar's penitential, canon law has become a silent but potent element of a penitential; and in time, it, not penitential handbooks, would emerge as predominant in dealing with issues of penances.

# Bibliography

Primary Sources

McNeill, John T. and Helena M. Gamer, eds. *Medieval Handbooks of Penance: A translation of the principal libri poenitentiales and selections from related documents.* New York: Columbia University Press, 1938.

MGH *Concilia*, vol. 1, 273-285 (Council of Chalons, 813)

MGH *Concilia*, vol. 2, 596-680 (Council of Paris, 829)

Migne. *Patrologia Latina* 105, 651D-710A (Halitgar's penitential)

_____. *Patrologia Latina* 119, 704-726 (Diocesan statute of Rudolph of Bourges, c. 850)


Secondary Sources

Connolly, Hugh. *The Irish Penitentials and their significance for the sacrament of penance today.* Portland: Four Courts Press, 1995.

Frantzen, Allen J. *The Literature of Penance in Anglo-Saxon England.* New Brunswick, New Jersey: Rutgers University Press, 1983.

Kottje, Raymond. *Die Bussbuecher Halitgars von Cambrai und des Hrabanus Maurus: Ihre Ueberlieferung und ihre Quellen.* Berlin, New York: Walter De Gruyter, 1980.

McNeill, John T. *Celtic Penitentials and Their Influence on Continental Christianity.* Paris: Librairie Ancienne Honore Champion, 1923.

Mordek, Hubert. "Kanonistische Activitaet in Gallien in der Ersten Haelfte des 8. Jahrhunderts," *Francia* 2 (1978), 19-25.

_____, ed. *Kirchenrecht und Reform im Frankenreich: Die Collectio Vetus Gallica, Die Aelteste Systematische Kanonessammlung Des Fraenkischen Gallien.* Berlin, New York: Walter De Gruyter, 1975.

Otten, Willemien. "The Texture of Tradition. The Role of the Church

Fathers in Carolingian Theology," *The Reception of the Church Fathers in the West: From the Carolingians to the Maurists*, vol. 1, ed. Irena Backus. Leiden, New York, Koeln: E. J. Brill, 1997, 3-50.

Payer, Pierre J. *Sex and the Penitentials: The Development of a Sexual Code 550-1150*. Toronto: University of Toronto Press, 1984.

Pelikan, Jaroslav. *The Growth of Medieval Theology (600-1300)*. Chicago: University of Chicago Press, 1978.

Reynolds, Roger E. "Unity and Diversity in Carolingian Canon Law Collections: The Case of the *Collectio Hibernensis* and Its Derivatives," *Carolingian Essays*, ed. Uta-Renate Blumenthal. Washington, D.C.: The Catholic University of America Press, 1983, 99-136.

Sheehy, Maurice. "Influences of Ancient Irish Law on *the Collectio Canonum Hibernensis*," *Proceedings of the Third International Congress of Medieval Canon Law*, ed. Stephan Kuttner, *Monumenta iuris canonici*, Ser. C, Subsidia 4. Citta del Vaticano: Biblioteca Apostolica

Vaticana, 1968, 31-42.

Werckmeister, Jean. "The Reception of the Church Fathers in Canon Law" *The Reception of the Church Fathers in the West: From the Carolingians to the Maurists*, vol. 1, ed. Irena Backus. Leiden, New York, Koeln: E. J. Brill, 1997, 51-82.

## About the Author

Onyoo Elizabeth Kim is Adjunct Professor of Law at Handong University Law School in Korea. She is licensed to practice law in the states of California, New Jersey, and Pennsyvlania. She received her J.D. degree from the UCLA Law School in 1997. In 1994, she graduated Phi Beta Kappa from the University of Pennsylvania with a B.A. and M.A. degree in history. She also had Latin as her second major.

Professor Kim has researched extensively on medieval law at UCLA, the University of Pennsylvania, Yale University, and the University of Cologne in Germany. She is also considered to be one of the leading experts on medieval Latin texts on law and criminal justice.

Professor Kim has worked in coporate law before joining the faculty of Handong University Law School in one of the leading Asian lawfirms, Woo, Yun, Kang, Jeong & Han in Seoul. She worked primarily with legal cases related to US and EU Constitutional Law and International Law. She is currently on staff at the lawfirm as research lawyer/legal consultant.

www.ingramcontent.com/pod-product-compliance
Lightning Source LLC
Chambersburg PA
CBHW030341240426
43661CB00052B/1706